THE REAL ESTATE AGENT SUCCESS SERIES

Three Powerful Best-Selling Books
Packed in One Convenient Book

William J. May

WILLIAM J. MAY

Disclaimer: William J. May is a licensed real estate agent in Torrance, California. Printed in the USA. The information presented herein represents the views of the author as of the date of publication. This book is presented for informational purposes only. This book contains statistical examples.

It is understood, if you use these statistics, you need to know your own market. Real Estate is local, and every market is different. Due to the rate of which conditions change, the author reserves the right to alter and/or update this information based on new conditions. While every attempt has been made to verify the information in this book, neither the author nor his affiliates/partners assume any responsibility for errors, inaccuracies, or omissions. It is understood that the income statements and examples are not intended to represent or guarantee that anyone will achieve the same results. Each individual's success will be determined by his or her desire, dedication, background, skills, knowledge, effort, and motivation to work and follow recommendations. There is no guarantee you will duplicate the results stated. You recognize any business endeavor has an inherent risk for loss of capital.

Top 10 Expired Objections

Know what words to say and when to say them.

Dedication

To Gwen –
The love of my life, my true north, my backbone to my success. With all my heart with all my love. Thank you for always being there for me and always reminding me, with the Lord's help, there's nothing that I cannot accomplish. Thank you.

Foreword

I first met William in a real estate group on Facebook. I remember seeing a post where he was making thousands of calls a week. At the time, I was lucky to hand dial 100 numbers a day.

I sent him a message and set up a call with him to see what he's doing. From then on we have been friends and talk regularly.

William is an expert in learning scripts, dialogues, and objections! When he told me he was writing this book and asked if I would write a foreword and give some advice, I told him I thought the idea for this book was excellent!

I think there should be more training material like this in the real estate industry.

Here is the best advice I can give you on learning to overcome objections when prospecting on the phone. The first thing many agents have to do is overcome the fear of getting on the phone. I really believe the best way for you to overcome the fear is to have a system that you can have
confidence in and practice as much as possible.

Part of that system is learning to overcome objections and practicing those objections over and over. I believe it is one of the basic fundamentals of the business.

The fundamentals are the boring things you do over and over every day. They are also the skills you need to win every day.

If you take this book and the information in it, find a roleplay partner and practice them over and over, I guarantee it will change your business. What I will do for you also is help you find a roleplay partner today! All you need to do is join my Facebook Group: Real estate agents that REALLY work and post:

"I just bought William May's book and I need a role play Partner".

You will get one ASAP.

Jason Morris
Real Estate Agents that Really Work
https://www.facebook.com/groups/RealEstateAgentsthatREALLYwork

P.S. I have a special gift I am going to give you. Actually, it is my #1 tool in my listing Tool Box. It is my Pre-listing package. Download it for free at http://bit.ly/2v6hWwx

Introduction

Expired listings, easy pickings, low hanging fruit, the number one source for successful Real Estate Agents to make a living...yeah OK, I have heard it all. So you're probably asking...

> "If this is the case, why aren't all Realtors jumping on the Expired Listing bandwagon since this is an easy source of business?"

The non-sugar-coated truth is...it's hard work! Trying to pull the expired listing from that low hanging vine will, in most cases, break your damn back. If not your back, then your spirit. So, I've decided to put pen to paper or fingers to keyboard and try to assist other Agents in working with expired listings.

When I first started in the business, I was using 30-year-old scripts. It seemed like the expired listings that I called knew what I was going to say, even before I said it. Not to mention, the expired person was pissed off because I wasn't the only Agent calling them at 8 o'clock in the morning.

I don't know where you practice Real Estate, but I'm sure competition across the country is fierce. I practice in Los Angeles, California. It seems like everyone and their mother has a Real Estate license. Even though my market is flooded with Real Estate Agents, in my experience, most Agents do not work expired listings.

If you put forth the effort to pick up this book, that means you're looking for something to help your Real Estate business to succeed. Let's imagine this for a moment...you're working with expired listings and you're closing deals. You have the confidence of a top producer. Why? Because you *are* a Top Producer.

There's no expired listing under the sun, that you cannot sell. Everyone at the office is looking up to you. You and your family can just go on vacation whenever you want. You have the house you want, the car you want, and the lifestyle you want. You have made up your mind to succeed, and you know the only way to fail in this business is by giving up or quitting.

At the beginning of my Real Estate career, my biggest challenge working with expired listings was picking up the phone and knowing what to say. Every successful Real Estate Agent starts at zero and with that uncertainty in the beginning.

Please do not let the title of this book fool you. Yes, I'll help you with the most common objection for expireds. But also, this book is crammed with a lot of useful information that's designed to help fellow Agents across the country deal with the most common objections and a few tips that helped me along the way.

This will be my first book in **The Real Estate Agent Success Series**. It is written by an Agent that is actually in the trenches, closing deals, working with clients, and getting the job done.

There's so many coaches and programs on the Internet, you'll go broke purchasing them all. I was once a new Agent struggling for knowledge, scared of the business, unsure of myself, wondering what to do next. that's exactly why I took the time to write this book. To help other Agents to succeed and to reassure them it is possible to be successful in Real Estate without taking you to the bank.

I hope this book will help you in your business and help those expired listings to finally get sold with your help. I would say "good luck", but with a positive attitude, determination, and consistency, you won't need it.

Go get them!

Working With Expired Listings

Like I mentioned earlier, it's been said expired listings are easy pickings or low-hanging fruit, and they are the number one source of business for most successful Agents that are willing to work them.

That may be the case, but if you ever talk to Agents who have been in the business for a while and do not work expired listings, they have a lot to say about them and it is mostly negative.

Veteran Agent: "Well you know, Sonny, those expired listings...they're not realistic on price; they are difficult people. If they did want to sell, they would be sold already!"

Its definitely one way to look at it, but I look at it like this: please do not take offense, but just maybe it might be the Agent's fault. Of course, the Agent wanted to sell the property and have a successful closing for his clients. This is how he/she makes his/her money and is able to feed his/her family. Everyone has to eat, right? Of course.

There's a lot of moving parts at play. Maybe the Agent couldn't handle the objections or the seller's unrealistic value of their property, so he/she listed the property too high. As a result, the property does not sell/expires. Perhaps the Agent didn't have a listing presentation strong enough to convey his/her professionalism that he/she knows what needs to be done to sell the property at the highest possible price.

It could have been a weak CMA or "Competitive Market Analysis" that it did not show the proper market value of the property. Another big problem I see with Agents is that they are commission-hungry. They are not presenting themselves as a Real Estate Professional. It could have been one or a mixture of all of these things.

Frankly, your job as a Real Estate Professional is to demonstrate to your client that you're the man or woman for the job. These are the comps in the neighborhood and the market is going to bear what the market is going to bare for the property. It is my job as your Real Estate Agent to get you the most money possible. In order for me to do that, we must work together so we can have a successful conclusion to the deal.

One thing I've learned from my wise and true broker:

"There's nothing wrong with a house that the right price won't fix."

For expired listings, prices are usually the number one reason why the property did not sell. Nine times out of ten, the seller wants way too much for their property. It's our job as professional Real Estate Agents to make sure that we demonstrate to our clients the best strategies to get their property sold without leading them into the expired wasteland.

Expired Listing and Agent Mindset

Working with expired listings, you must have a certain kind of mindset. You also must understand your potential expired client mindset as well.

Remember this, if you don't remember anything else:

"It's your own mindset that determines your success in Real Estate or not."

Expired Mindset

Depending on when you're going to interact with the expired determines their mindset in most cases. It's always a good idea to be ready to work early in the morning. Be ready to start calling at 7:45 or 8 o'clock.

Believe me, it's always best to learn from someone else's mistakes. I was always under the impression that expired listings in Los Angeles were rude, crazy, or just outright insane people. If these people really wanted to sell, they would be sold by now. Absolutely something must be wrong with these people. "Of course, they're expired!" I said to myself.

The reason I had that impression is because by the time I got on the phones and started prospecting at 9,10, or 11 o'clock in the morning, they had already been contacted by so many other Agents that they were pissed off. **No wonder!** That's why they were cussing me out, hanging up in my face, not wanting to be bothered with me or anyone else that mentions Real Estate! I can't tell you how many times I heard this from different trainers:

"You must be the first one in the morning to contact expired listings."

Agent Mindset

Playing the expired prospecting game, you must be aware of your own mindset. Of course, we understand that the expired listing is going to be upset that their home did not sell. This might sound crazy, but this is a good thing. You may ask why is this a good thing? Motivation! The homeowner still wants to sell their home and move.

This is where you stick out your chest, raise your head up high, and speak with authority with confidence.

Your affirmation:

"I'm a Top Expired Listing Specialist and I help people! Who's next?"

Have the mindset that you are a Real Estate Professional. I can help this homeowner sell their home and net them more money than any other Agent.

I didn't realize it then, but I now know how important it is to be one of the first Agents or the first Agent to contact expired listings in the morning.

One week, I decided to start prospecting an hour earlier in the morning, so I started calling at 8 o'clock. I noticed right off the bat, for the first 30 minutes of my prospecting, that I started having actual conversations with expireds. The rest is history.

From that morning on, I've been calling expired listings starting at 7:45 or 8 o'clock in the morning. I have a total mind shift when it comes to working with expired listings now. Understand I'm not saying just because I'm calling them earlier that it's easy pickings. No, it's still hard work, but I learned something very valuable that 90% of the Real Estate Agents don't know or don't realize:

From 7:45 to 8:30 is probably the absolute best time to have a beneficial conversation with a new expired listing.

My strategy is:
1. Find out their motivation
2. Get their information
3. Set an appointment
4. Follow up

Very rarely does an expired call become a list for me. You must have the mindset that you have to follow up with them consistently to develop a relationship. In this way, you build rapport so you can close the business when it makes sense for them.

Do Not Ever Be Commission Hungry

A commission-hungry vulture of a Real Estate Agent...that's all he wants to do is close another sale at the client's expense. Clients can always smell this a mile away. You're a professional. You know what you're doing, and without you, they will not be able to walk away from the closing table with the most money possible.

If you understand where the expired client mindset is coming from, you're already ahead of the game because you know they're going to be upset that their house didn't sell. They were unable to move on with their plans and now they have a million and one Agents calling for their home driving them crazy. Your main goal is not to get the listing on the first contact. your main goal is to see if you can help.

To help, you have to go through a good expired script. In this way, you can check their motivation and, in most cases, obtain useful information that you can use to help them make a decision that will best help their family. Through the conversation, if it looks like you can help, you would want to set an appointment to meet or at least see the property. In this way, you can at least have an opportunity to meet the potential client face-to-face.

There's nothing better than belly-to-belly, face-to-face meetings in sales. I tell you there's nothing more uplifting than you helping people and getting paid for it.

Always remember:

"If you look out for their best interest it will serve you well."

Frequently Asked Questions

Where do I get the numbers?

There are several different services to get expired listings or numbers in general. There are not as many landlines as there used to be. Just keep in mind, every year the lines get fewer and fewer.

I've tried several different expired listing services. In my opinion, you would have to try various services and see which service works best in your market.

A list of Expired Listing services in no particular order:

1. Red X - http://www.theredx.com/expireds/
2. Landvoice.com - https://landvoice.com/expireds/
3. Vulcan7.com - https://www.vulcan7.com/
4. ReboGateway.com - http://www.rebogateway.com/intro/home
5. MojoSells.com - http://www.mojosells.com/ (I personally use and endorse)
6. EspressoAgent.com - https://espressoagent.com/expireds/

If you would like to look some up yourself. Here are some sites I have used.

Bonus
Spokeo.com, Intelius.com, Dexknows.com

What is the best expired training course?

If you check the Internet, you will probably see a quite few expired listing programs out there on the market. In my personal opinion, Borino Expired Plus (https://expiredplus.com/) is the best.

The reason why I feel his course is so beneficial to new and existing Real Estate Agents is because the creator learned in one of the hardest markets to be successful in Southern California.

Also, his program is not just fluff, but hours and hours of continuous, relevant content that is updated constantly. If you don't believe me, check his YouTube Channel (https://www.youtube.com/channel/UCL5mptC7KYHmx10xWZXokng) or his

Facebook Group: https://www.facebook.com/groups/rockstar.agents/. See how his students are kicking Real Estate A$$!

Like I mentioned before, there are tons of expired listing programs on the market. I know quite a few, but I only suggest the ones I've tried personally.

I cannot stress this enough: I don't want new Agents or existing Agents to go through what I went through...getting robbed blind by so-called Real Estate gurus selling you on the latest silver bullet or new magic pill. If I've told you once, I've told you a thousand times, there's no silver bullet or magic pill to be successful in Real Estate. Only hard work, determination, and consistency will lead you to success in anything you do.

What is the best auto dialer to use?

You have Turbodial for Infusionsoft, Vulkan 7, Red Storm Dialer, and quite a few others. The whole purpose of using an auto-dialer is to be more efficient in your prospecting. There are many types of auto-dialers. Some have a single line while others have a multi-line set up.

If you're a new Agent or just starting out calling expired listings, I would suggest you start with the old-fashioned method. Use your cell phone or office phone. These are high-quality leads. You do not want to lose the expired listing because of a bad or delayed connection.

When you're new at calling expired listings, it's best to get comfortable with calling them one at a time. Do not rush it. Take your time. If you work them in this way, your comfort level and experience will increase. Only then would I suggest using an auto-dialer.

My auto-dialer of choice is the Mojo Sales Dialer. I can cold-call/circle prospect with three lines at a time. The system can call through 300 numbers per hour. It is a tremendous time-saver over calling one at a time on your own phone. And for an added bonus, if I don't have that many numbers to call, I can adjust the dialing system to two lines or even just one.

Another reason why I like Mojo: in their system, you can set up groups. I have three groups for expired listings: New Expires, Prime Expires, and Old Expires.

New Expired

New expired listings are from 0 to 14 days. When I call through these listings, I will hand-dial these numbers or use the Mojo one-line dialer. This is more efficient than using the multi-line dialer on these leads.

Prime Expired

Prime Expired listings are from day 15 to 3 months. When I call through the prime expired list, I use the two-line dialer. This group tends to have a few more numbers than the New Expireds group. I usually call this list several times because from 14 to 3 months is usually where you get the most expired listings or turn over. That means they probably will list with you if you have good follow-up. Sometimes, they have already listed with another Agent.

Old Expired

Old Expired listings are from 3 months and beyond. I use the three-line dialer when I'm calling through the old expireds. As you can imagine, I have a ton of old expired numbers in this group. If they do not relist or tell me to take them off my list, I will keep them in that Old Expired group.

If you don't use Mojo, you can still use this system or a variation of the system on any other dialer/database system.

What is the best CRM to use?

So, what is the best Customer Relationship Management System (CRM) to use? Well, the short and crazy answer is whatever CRM you're comfortable in using. There are so many programs out there, I'm not even going to begin to try to list them.

What I would suggest if you're a new Agent, and you've made up your mind on which expired system to use to retrieve your data, it's a pretty good bet that the expired system would be the best CRM system to start with. You're familiar with it, and you know how it works. That's the system you're going to be using on a daily basis.

If you're an Agent that's been in the game for a while and tired of your current CRM, experiment with different CRM's that are out there. Usually, they'll have a free trial or some kind of promotion to get your precious business.

Okay okay, I'll name a few:

- Top Producer - http://www.topproducer.com/products/top-producer-crm
- Red X - http://www.theredx.com/
- MojoDialer - http://www.mojosells.com/
- Infusionsoft - https://www.infusionsoft.com/product/features/small-business-crm
- Salesforce - https://www.salesforce.com/
- BoomTown - https://boomtownroi.com/features/predictive-crm/

...and on and on and on. You get the picture.

Well William, what CRM do you use? I actually use two CRM's. Yes, I'm crazy like that. The truth is, for right now it's best for me to use two CRM's in my business. Eventually, that may change. Like I mentioned earlier, you have to treat your business like a living, growing business. When it grows, you must grow with it.

I used the Mojo Dialer and Contactually.
(http://try.contactually.com/)

I have to give Mojo credit in the last few years they have developed into a very powerful CRM with a three-line dialer. I'm not going to go into detail. I primarily use Mojo for the dialing system. To circle prospect/cold-calling, expired, For Sale By Owners, and My People Farm.

Contactually is the second CRM that I use for the simple interface and the ease-of-use. I primarily use Contactually for working my Spear of Influence (SOI) and my database. Unfortunately, Contactually doesn't have a dialing system, but I wouldn't hold that against them.

Just take your time. Do your own due diligence. See which program best fits you, your business, and your personality.

Should I leave a message?

Should I, or shouldn't I leave a message? That is the great debate amongst Real Estate Agents. I will tell you this: if you do not leave a message you're one hundred percent guaranteed not to receive a call back regarding your message.

In my experience when I first started cold-calling without a dialer, leaving messages took a lot of my time. However, I received two great listings from cold-calling and one I was able to double end. Leaving messages is like the lottery. You don't win unless you play!

As far as working with expired listings: if you have some experience calling them, you will notice after a few hours or days that the expired voicemail becomes full. For the first 24 to 48 hours the homeowner's phone is probably ringing off the hook. They're mad, upset, and frustrated. In some cases, they turn off or unplug the phone. So an answering machine does all the work for them by screening the calls that come in.

Personally, I do not leave a message during the first few days. This is my decision. I know several Real Estate Agents that leave messages on the first and second calls. Remember back at the beginning of this book when I'm talked about the expired mindset?

They're getting bombarded with calls and messages. Yes, I'm among the Agents who are calling the expired listing when it first hits my computer screen. I'm trying to actually reach the potential client so I can help them out of their situation. When I'm calling through the numbers again after about a week or so, that's when I use the Mojo Dialer to drop a voicemail to the expired listing. By this time, the craziness has subsided somewhat, and they're not so angry or hostile. In most cases, they are more open to actually return an Agent's phone call.

How should I follow up with Expireds?

It basically depends on the expired itself. Each one is different in its own way. Studies have shown that expired listings usually relist within three weeks. If you're lucky enough to actually speak with them and they say they definitely need to sell their home, follow up is mandatory!

I'm sure you've heard "money is in the follow up"?

There are several ways to follow up. So, this is the down and dirty version:

1. **Make the first initial call.** If no answer, call two or three times a day for two weeks. In this way, you're cleaning your list from bad numbers, wrong numbers, and the Do-Not-Call List. At the end of the first week if you have not made contact, leave a message if possible. (Remember to rotate through the different phone numbers you call out on.)

2. **You made contact.** Congratulations! These contacts can fall into several different categories, but for this book, we're keeping it simple. Follow-up. Remember the 80/20 rule. The majority of the people you call or speak with are going to result in some sort of issue. Just understand that's part of the business: the Game of Expireds. Shake it off, and move on. We have some money to make.

   If you have a nice decent conversation, but they're not sure when they're going to relist, ask when is the best time to check back. Whatever they say, cut that in half. After you get off the phone, send a thank you card. Make mention of something about the conversation: the reason why they're moving, where they're going, or how you can help, etc.

   Whatever database you're using, make sure you give them a call a week later to see if they got your card. What you're doing is building rapport. If you're able to get their email address, then send them your information that same day, and put them on a monthly email drip campaign with market stats or something else of value.

3. **The best way is always in person.** Have a mini resume (which I use from the Barino Expired Plus system) handy, or something of value that shows that you're a professional and you have testimonials of satisfied clients. If you're new in the business and do not yet have past sales, speak with your broker about using the brokerage sales stats. When I was new in the business, I had to make do with what I had at the time. Remember, you always have to crawl before you can walk.

Where do I find good roleplay partners?

To be a master at your craft of communicating, role-playing your scripts plays an essential part in developing your skills. You can lose tens of thousands of dollars on what you say or what you don't say.

Your communication skills are like a muscle. You must work it out every day, every week, and every month. At some point, they'll be a part of you, ingrained in you. Your words will be who you are.

You might be one of those who say, "I don't like scripts, it doesn't sound right, it's not me."

Did you ever come to think that every time you pick up a phone and say "hello", that's a script? What is your favorite movie of all time? No matter what the answer is, I guarantee you the actors that played in that movie, all worked with scripts.

The best thing about scripts is that they're totally evolving. You'll learn the basic scripts, and those basic scripts you will build into more advanced scripts. And as you practice and internalize these scripts, they become a part of you. This takes hours and hours of practicing, rehearsing, and real-world experience.

I would suggest that you find a good roleplay partner in Jason Morris' Facebook Group (https://www.facebook.com/groups/RealEstateAgentsthatREALLYwork).

At the time of this publication, the group is close to 20,000 members ready and willing to share information on prospecting, marketing, and role-playing. It's not uncommon in the group to get multiple answers from Agents all around the country that are actually successful in Real Estate.

Is memorizing my scripts enough to be successful?

Knowing the script and dialogues is not enough. You need to adapt to the prospect the same way as a boxer bobs and weaves during a fight not to get hit. Understand you have control over your destiny. As a matter of fact, you need to understand your action goals and your result goals. It's been said many times Real Estate is a numbers game. So understanding your result goals and number goals will help you achieve this.

You might say a result goal is saying "I'm going to set up one appointment a day". That is something you don't have control over but you do have control over your action goals.

Action goals might be something like making up your mind to have the discipline to prospect three hours a day; five days a week. You definitely have control over your action goals. If you continue with the actions, it will build up like The Compound Effect. Once you start taking listings, you'll start generating momentum.

The more prospecting that you do, the better you will get with your communication (scripts and dialogues). The more interaction you have with your clients, the better you will become with your customer service. The more people you help, the more deals you will close.

Sometimes it's not what you say, or how you say it. Sometimes the hardest part is, just picking up the phone and making that first call. I'm sure you understand now, an Agent that works expired listings understands there is a method to the madness.

Objections vs. Conditions

Objections vs. Conditions, what's the difference between the two? Well, it's pretty simple really.

Example of an Objection:
An Objection is basically an obstacle to overcome. Either the client needs more information on something or does not trust you. They could just be trying to blow you off. Your job as a Real Estate Professional is to determine which one it is.

Let's say, for example, a client asks you:

"How many homes have you sold in my area?"

In my opinion, this is clearly a sign of no connection with the seller. You need to establish rapport or a connection with the seller to show them that you're a professional and that you sell homes. Not only that you sell homes, but you sell them faster, and for more money than your competition.

You have to understand that, if the seller decides to use you they are most likely putting the most expensive Real Estate asset they own in your hands. So don't be surprised if the seller is asking you qualifying questions until they feel comfortable and confident that they are making the right decision.

In this example, you can use your numbers or if you're new, you can use your company's area sales. Always be familiar with your numbers and your company's numbers so this way you are always on top of your game.

Example:
Seller: How many homes have you sold in my area?

You: Mr. Seller, I'm happy to let you know, in the last 60 days WE have sold over 38 properties. I'm not saying this to impress you, but to impress upon you, that out of 38 closed sales, we have sold 23 of those properties over asking price. You would agree with me, this type of service would be beneficial to you and your family,.correct?

After they say yes.... go for the close!

Example of a Close:
You: Mr. Seller let's do this...my schedule books up pretty quickly. Let's get something on the calendar. What works best for your schedule? Later on this week, early afternoon or would the evenings or weekend be better for your schedule?

Tip: You will notice throughout this book. When it comes to handling objections. I repeat, affirm, and ask another question. When I'm giving examples, I try to have several different closes and several different responses. This way, you're not saying the same thing over and over again sounding like a robot.

Example of a Condition:
A condition, on the other hand, is basically a bridge you cannot cross or a wall you cannot climb over. Conditions are an immediate roadblock when communicating with a client or a potential client.

Understand, just like an objection, there are different kinds of conditions. Most will derail your plans immediately, but some can resolve over time.

For instance...

Seller: Yes, Mr. May, we're definitely going to sell our house but not until our son graduates from high school this coming June.

This is an immediate condition you cannot do anything about. But on the other hand, this is still a high-value lead. Stay in contact and offer them things of value. You should be able to convert them when the time is right.

Another example of the condition...

Seller: Yes, Mr. May, I would love to sell, but I just can't sell and pay off my tax lien and have money to move on with my life. The numbers do not work out.

This is another example of a condition. Unless the potential client comes up with the finances to pay off the tax lien or his property value rises enough for him to move forward, there's nothing you can do in this situation. In this situation, I would put the client in my People Farm and definitely stay in touch. Maintaining and growing that relationship with follow-up will generate referrals for you in the future. **The money is in the follow-up!**

The sooner you identify an objection or condition, the sooner you know which direction to proceed with the lead. I can only give you an outline, definition, or my own experience. Always remember each market is different, so the best advice comes with your own experience.

Consistency

In every part of your Real Estate career, you must have consistency, especially in your prospecting. You need to set a schedule every day where you prospect, follow up, and go on appointments on a consistent basis. Your Real Estate career depends on it.

This may sound crazy or absurd, but you have to think of your Real Estate career as a **Living Breathing Business** that you constantly have control over.

There is a saying in Real Estate:

"The leads you generate today will feed you and your family for three months, six months, and up to a year from now."

Think of your Real Estate career as a business, and your Real Estate business as a job. You are the star employee of your business. Since you are also the owner/operator of your successful Real Estate business, you have a business plan in place. You also have a set business schedule you follow each workweek.

In order to do this on a successful, consistent basis, you must set up a schedule or routine and stick to it.

For example, let's say your schedule for prospecting is Monday through Friday from 8 AM to 11:30 AM. This is the designated time for you to call all of your prospects like new expireds and old expireds, FSBO, SOI, database, and follow-ups. You get the idea.

From 11:30 to 1 PM you have your lunch and run errands.

From 1 o'clock to 6 PM can be a mixture of things that could change daily. Regardless, you should be doing prospecting or lead nurturing activities during this time such as:

- Follow-up
- Calling back expireds or For Sale By Owners
- Working on your afternoon appointments

In my experience, setting listing appointments ranges between 2 o'clock or 5 o'clock in the afternoon. Very seldom am I taking listing appointments later than that. If you're starving realtor or you need to jumpstart your business again, take the listing at whatever time the client is available and willing to meet with you.

The Weekend

If you're a new Real Estate Agent or just need to jump-start your business, work every single weekend you can get your hands on. Weekends are the best days to generate business. Nine times out of ten, more people are home on the weekends than any other day of the week.

You can do open houses, door-knocking, or phone prospecting. The best thing to do is to get face-to-face, belly-to-belly with as many potential customers as you can. Once you have a steady flow of income, then take the weekends off so you can spend more time with your family. That's priceless!

It's a Numbers Game!

One thing I love about Real Estate is that it's dependable and predictable. If you work hard enough and long enough, eventually you will succeed. The only way you will not succeed in Real Estate is if you give up, throw in the towel, or call it quits. In this business, you have to have consistency to win.

Real estate is a game you can win. Do not let anyone tell you otherwise... even yourself. You made it this far, you can go all the way. Did you know the numbers are in your favor? Did you know that homeowners are **70% more likely to use the first Agent that they come in contact with?** It sounds like good news to me.

Before I go deep, I would like to tell you a quick story of the sower. Most likely you have probably heard of this story of a farmer who is planting seeds. One day, the farmer walks around his farm scattering seeds in different places.

One area of the farm where the seeds were scattered, the birds came quickly and ate the seeds. Some fell on the rocks with light soil and began to grow, but on the first hot day they died off. Other seeds fell in the thorns and as the seeds began to grow, the thorns choked the life out of them. Some seeds fell on rich, good ground and produced a good crop for the farmer.

The purpose of this story is to explain that prospecting is a numbers game, or what you can call the law of averages. You might have even heard of the 80-20 rule. It all boils down to you knowing your numbers. Numbers don't lie.

Do you remember earlier in the book when I mentioned you have a living business in Real Estate? Knowing your numbers plays a huge role in having a successful business.

So let's talk numbers! When you call expireds, keep track of your numbers. This way, over time you have a track record to review. Let's say, for example, an experienced expired listing specialist finds a listing after speaking to 80 people. On the other hand, an Agent with not so much experience working expireds might take the listing after talking to 160 people or more. Let's go even deeper. A brand new Agent might not even take a listing at all after talking to more than 300 expired listings.

You have to put all the pieces together to have the numbers work in your favor. What do I mean by this? Practice, practice, and more practice. Take the time every day to practice your scripts and dialogues.

You may not understand this, but this is an investment in your future. The more expireds you talk to, the more comfortable you get with speaking to them and the more you realize they all have the same objections.

When you start out, prospecting expireds is going to be hard and daunting. Please understand this is a normal process. To become successful, you have to crawl before you can walk. You have to walk before you can run. It might take you two weeks, a month, or six months to become proficient in dealing with expireds.

I want you to know you have several things in common with successful mega Agents. We all put our shoes on one foot at a time. At some point, we all started at zero. The cool thing about this whole process is it's only going to be difficult in the beginning, but once you start becoming used to the process, it will get easier and easier.

When you first start calling expireds, you are going to realize a lot of people are going to be upset, angry, and frustrated. That's only normal when they listed the house with an Agent that didn't get the job done for whatever reason. That derailed their plans. Of course, you would be upset too if you wanted to move and weren't able to. So if you understand their mindset, you are more likely to be in a position to not take their frustration personally. It's part of the Real Estate game like I said before.

I don't understand how a lot of these coaches and trainers throw out these ridiculous numbers like, "for every ten expireds you call, you get one listing," or something ridiculous like that. I believe in real-world numbers and it's not pretty. It's not meant to be. Being successful, like I said, is hard work.

These numbers are just an example of the worst-case scenario. As you know, your results may vary. Once you start the process and get more familiar with your prospecting style and contact ratio, the numbers will develop a pattern that you can use to build your business for success.

Let's say you have to dial 100 numbers to get two contacts.

Let's say you need 100 contacts to generate two good leads.

Let's say you need fifty leads to generate one appointment.

Finally, let's say you take three appointments to get one listing.

As you look at these numbers, that might get you a little nervous but it gives you an idea of how to manage your business based on what you need to do. As you prospect expireds and get more familiar with them, and follow up with them, your numbers will improve. Your confidence will increase, your conversions will start taking off, you'll start taking more listings, and closing transactions because you embraced working with the numbers.

The farmer had to manage his crop the same way you have to manage your prospects. When you call an expired and they're not ready, now you have to nurture that prospect, stay in front of them, send them things of value, and answer their questions. Of course, you're going to lose most of the time: they're going to tell you not call them anymore or that they're on the Do-Not-Call list.

You might have a good conversation with them since you built a little rapport. However, like some of the seeds that fell on the stony ground, next time you look up, they listed with another Agent. It will happen to you. It happens to the best of us.

With the select few that you stay in consistent contact and follow up with, they will come to understand your U.V.P. (Unique Value Proposition). They will value your service and list their home with you. After the smoke clears and the dust settles, you will have a successful closing with a satisfied client for life. Priceless!

Tools of the Trade

Your Calendar

Whether it's a physical calendar or digital calendar, your calendar is one of the main tools for being successful in Real Estate. Become accustomed to scheduling everything in your calendar. Spending time with the family, your family vacations, anything and everything must go into the calendar so you can stay on track with your business.

Make sure you schedule your prospecting as a recurring appointment. Do not schedule your listing appointments during prospecting hours. The only exception to the rule is, if you're new or you're in a sales slump, then, of course, drop everything and get that listing!

The end game is to make your business grow and to make money. Once you start taking listings, you will start closing listings. You will start generating momentum. Once that occurs, you will start doing what top Agents do: schedule their appointments away from prospecting hours. Soon enough, you will see yourself as a top-producing Agent.

Workstation

You need a quiet, distraction-free work environment. This could be your work office, home office, or just a quiet room with no distractions. If you have a designated workstation such as your office, the main thing you need to do before you start prospecting is turn off all social media, email, TV, and put your cell phone on airplane mode if you're not using it. Anything and everything that will distract you. Oh yes, do not forget to put the do-not-disturb sign on your doorknob.

Computer or Laptop

In this tech-savvy world. I don't see how it's even possible to have a Real Estate business without a computer. The computer or laptop doesn't have to be state-of-the-art and have all the bells and whistles known to man as long as you have a digital device that will help you prospect. I mainly work off of my home PC. At the office, I use my laptop. It's very mobile and convenient when I have to pick up and go to a conference room or to a meeting in another Agent's office.

I also use an iPad on the go. This is very convenient for me for several reasons. I could use it in a meeting or at a business lunch. I can conduct general prospecting on-the-go where I can log into my Mojo dialing system or into my CRM. Also, I take it with me on listing presentations. Just in case I need to show them any detail on comparable sales in the area.

Telephone

You must have a good, reliable cell phone. I would suggest a smartphone.
Don't hold it against me, but I am an Android type of guy. I do know of other successful Agents who use Apple phones as well.

Whatever brand you choose, make sure that you have a dependable service provider. It doesn't make sense for you to have a $1,000 phone that you can't use to make a ten-cent phone call or not have a good Internet connection. It's just not worth it.

Your Car

Your automobile is probably the most valuable piece of prospecting equipment that you will ever own. You can call, email, snail mail, text, or send smoke signals. Whatever form of prospecting you decide to do, there is nothing more valuable than being face-to-face, belly-to-belly with a potential client.

If you take the time to survey expired listings as I have done, you will see this time and time again if you ask them.

You: Mr./Mrs. Seller, the three weeks your home has been off the market, how many phone calls have you received from Agents?
Seller: Thousands.
You: Besides myself, how many Agents have actually come to your door?
Seller: Just you.

As you can see, you don't have to be a rocket scientist or a genius to figure out all you have to do.

Do what other Agents are not willing or too lazy to do to be successful in Real Estate.

Let me be the first to warn you: when you pull up to your first expired listing, the hardest part is getting out of the car. Once you make contact, you'll see the fear that you built up in your head was just unnecessary drama.

You will be asking yourself: why wasn't I doing this sooner?

Rules of Engagement

Are you ready to get down and dirty with expired objection handling?

Great, let me explain a few things to you. There's no magic bullet. There's no magic words or miraculous script that will make clients fall at your feet and beg you to sign the listing agreement. Even if you were born the silver-tongued devil himself, there's no way to convince someone to sell a high-ticket item such as a single-family residence without motivation.

Yeah, you could probably convince someone to buy a candy bar that your kid is selling from school. I can guarantee you this, there's no way you can persuade somebody to buy a house or to sell their house when they don't want to. Don't even try.

Most Agents don't understand we're not here just to collect a paycheck. We are here to service our clients. That primarily includes moving mountains, jumping over roadblocks, and God only knows what else. So basically, our job is making the Real Estate transaction as seamless as possible so they can move forward with their lives.

We are problem solvers. If they're looking to move up, move down, or go sideways, we're here to solve whatever problems they may have. We are here to help them sell their house for the most money possible.

Do not let your client expire in the first place

This goes without saying. Maybe I should say it just so you know that whatever you do, try your best not to have your client's property expire. In most cases when a property expires, the Agent has done a disservice to their clients.

I know every time a property expires, it's not the Agent's fault. As Real Estate Professionals, it's our job to educate our clients and have them understand that we are the professional, and the information that we're providing will get their home sold in the shortest amount of time with the most money in their pocket.

I have found that there are several ways to connect with expired sellers, or anyone for that matter, using different systems. NLP is one of them. NLP stands for Neuro-Linguistic Programming. If you talk to different Real Estate Agents, they have their own take on NLP. Once you get the basics down, it will help you connect and interact with your clients on a deeper emotional level.

Another system I like to use is the DISC profiles. DISC profiles consist of four key traits which are:

1. Dominance
2. Influencing
3. Steadiness
4. Compliance

When it comes to selling Real Estate, these traits have to be learned in order to communicate with people in ways they will best respond to you. I suggest you go online and take a DISC assessment test for yourself.

Education is always key. If you want to be successful in Real Estate, you have to upgrade your education. So, take the time to learn NLP and the DISC profile system. In doing this, you will become more knowledgeable and more successful than the average Real Estate Agent.

Consistency

We talked about this in an earlier chapter. Always be consistent in everything you do in your Real Estate business.

Never, never, never argue with a potential client!

I learned a long time ago always agree, agree, agree, and agree. Even if you disagree, you better agree! Some people just want to start an argument, and it's funny to me when they try to argue with me and I agree with them. They're stumped.

Let me clarify, this doesn't mean I'm agreeing to whatever they are saying. I *validate and agree* with them and move on with the conversation. You have to realize that some people are stuck on stupid or have just made up their minds on what they believe. When you run across a person like this, you have to make an educated decision about when is the best time to just move on.

I could tell you this, but you have to learn from your own experience. Working with difficult people is not worth it. Believe me when I tell you that you want to work with people who know you, like you, and trust you rather than someone that doesn't believe you're worth what you charge. These types of people will not accept your professional opinion regarding their property, and just don't have faith in your proven system to get their home sold for the most amount of money.

At the beginning of my Real Estate career, I was working with my Pastor from childhood. He knew me quite well. He also knew I was new in the business. I guess because he was in the military, he was used to getting his way. There were quite a few times we bumped heads. I learned a lot from that experience I was always professional when he brought up my inexperience in the business and how he sold properties before.

I informed him that after the great foreclosure crisis, a lot of things had changed. Even though I may not have had the experience as a veteran Real Estate Agent, I studied very hard and passed my Real Estate exam on the first try. The State of California Department of Real Estate issued me my salesman's license soon after. With the help of the number one brokerage, two top brokers, and 150 Agents at my office, I have more than enough experience to fall back on if I need it in order to sell your property for top dollar.

It came to the point where I had to tell him I cared about our friendship so much that I was willing to sacrifice our business relationship so that we could remain friends. I told him that he had my permission, to find a Real Estate Agent that was a better fit for him and his needs. There were no hard feelings, and to this day, we're still friends.

At the beginning of my career, I was kind of slow with firing difficult and crazy people. But now if I feel that I cannot help them and we do not see eye-to-eye, I let them go quick, fast, and in a hurry. In my Real Estate career, I've had many coaches and trainers.

Bob Loeffler taught me this:

It's not my job
To make crazy people sane,
Stupid people smart,
Mean people nice.
It's my job to find...
Nice, Sane, Smart People...
That I can help, and do business with.

As I look back on that experience, I did not know anything about NLP or the DISC profiles. Who knows what would have happened if I knew then what I know now.

There's another saying in Real Estate:

"Some of your best listings are the ones you don't take."

What is your (U.V.P) Unique Value Proposition?

Seller: What is my unique value proposition? Or why should I hire you?

You: Well, I specialize in selling expired homes other Agents were not able to sell. I'm like a Real Estate doctor. I examine the expired listing, how was it was listed, pictures, description, everything.

Step two, I communicate with the seller, check their motivation to see if they're realistic on price, see if I would be comfortable working with them, preview their property, and see if their property is in sellable condition in relation to the sale price.

Once I have all the information and review all the facts regarding the property, I will give them a plan of action on how we can sell their house, make the home show-ready, and available to potential buyers. I will have the property cleaned and staged, update the MLS with current information, professional photos, and a detailed description of the property and the neighborhood including the city to draw in buyers.

In most cases, you will price the home at a lower price. This is not always the case, but most of the time, that is the reason the home expired in the first place. It's our job as professional Real Estate Agents not to be involved in Real Estate malpractice by not having the strength of will or the professionalism, to be honest with the seller regarding price.

Demonstrate to the seller that you can do more than put a sign in the yard that's a different color, and you actually have a proven system to get their expired listing sold. This is your unique U.V.P!

Top 10 Objections

There is definitely a method to the madness. No matter what script you decide to use, your goal is the same:

Generate appointments. Determine if this lead is worth following up, or if the lead is trash.

Always repeat, affirm, and ask another question. Mirror and match the client. Let the potential client speak 80% of the time, and you, 20% of the time with questions. Statistics have shown the more someone talks, the more rapport you build. Focus on their needs and wants while keeping the end game in mind.

Top 10 Objections:

1. You're the 15th Agent to call me today!
2. Where were you when my house was on the market?
3. Do you have a buyer for my house?
4. We're going to list with the same Agent.
5. We're going to list with a new Agent.
6. We're going to take a break from the market and wait a while.
7. How are you different from my last Agent?
8. We changed our minds about selling/We're not selling!
9. What's your commission?
10. My last Agent said he'll cut his commission, will you?

1. You're the 15th Agent to call me today!

Response A

You: Wow..... I'm the 15th Agent to give you a call this morning? Do you know what I have in common with those other Agents?

Seller: No what?

You: They see the same thing I see: a beautiful home, that should have sold! What do you think stopped your home from selling?

Response B

You: You don't say, 15 Agents? Well, I can't speak for those other Agents, but your past Agent never informed me about your property. Let me ask you...how did you happen to pick your last Agent?

Response C

You: Wow Mr. Seller, that's a lot of Agents to be calling you all at once. I don't know about you, but if it were me, I'd be pissed off that my house did not sell and now all these Agents are calling me out of the blue. Mr. Seller, I know you are probably overwhelmed right now, but if you were able to get this home sold and move on with your plans, would you still want to do it?

2. Where were you when my house was on the market?

Golden Nugget:

This is the number one example of why I say you should be one of the first ones to call the homeowner when their listing expires. If you're the first one that calls them and they're upset because their previous Agent did not sell their home, that's usually a telltale sign that they have high motivation for selling and moving. If you wait until later on that morning or that afternoon and you're the 500th Agent calling asking for the listing, it's safe to say they're pissed off because you're blowing up their phone. In their eyes, you're just like everyone else...a vulture Real Estate Agent trying to get the listing!

Response A

You: Working like a dog. Did you know, Mr./Mrs. Seller, at the same time that your property was on the market, we sold over 35 homes. Let me ask Mr. Seller, I know your time is valuable, were you just looking to list your property or actually get your property sold!?

Seller: Yes sold. (sample of a close I use)

You: Exactly, this is all I'm proposing. I would like to go over three things with you. First, I would like to pop by and show you exactly why your home did not sell. Second, I would like to show you a few things that will definitely draw in buyers interested to pay top dollar for your home. Mr. Seller, would you say that's pretty important?

Seller: Yes.

You: Finally, the third thing is I'm going to show you why my homes sell for top dollar. We can get together real quick today at 3 PM or 5 PM or I have a 4 PM and a 6:30 PM tomorrow if that would be better for your schedule?

Response B

You: Working for my clients. An Agent's job is to generate the highest level of buyers to buy your home and get it sold. That was not the case for you. What will you expect from the next Agent you choose?

Response C

You: I can understand your frustration. You had your home on the mark for _____ months and only now the Agents come out of the woodwork. Let me ask, if you can still get your price and get your home sold in 30 to 45 days would you still sell it?

3. Do you have a buyer for my house?

Response A

You: You know what, that's a good question. I don't know. I haven't seen your house yet. Are you still interested in selling?

Response B

You: I don't know. Our office has over fifty Agents that work with an average of three buyers each. If we can generate a full price offer and get you sold, that would definitely work for you and your family...right?

Response C

You: Let me ask, what type of buyer are you looking for? (No matter what they say...) Okay, we can agree the best buyer is someone that is ready and willing to pay your price and can close escrow.

If I/we can generate that buyer and get you back on track with your original plans are you ready to put us to work?

4. We're going to list with the same Agent.

Response A
You: I can understand that. So, you're going with the same Agent, is that correct?
Seller: Yes.
You: Okay let me ask you this, is 15 or 20 minutes of your time worth possibly saving 15 to 20 thousand of your equity?

Response B
You: I can definitely understand that. Let me ask, what will your Agent do this time around to definitely get your home sold?

Response C
You: I can understand stand that, you were on the market for over a half a year. I don't know about you, but to me, that's a long time. If I can show you a proven plan that I use to sell homes for top dollar. Would you like to hear more about it?

Response D
You: What can you possibly lose by spending 15-20 minutes with me?

Response E
You: What can you possibly lose by getting a second opinion on your most valuable asset?

Response F
You: What can you possibly lose by getting a second opinion with a powerful Agent such as myself. You do want to get the most money for your home, right?

Response G
You: What's most important to you in an Agent?

Response H
You: What is it about that other Agent that makes you want to stay with them?

Response I

You: What's more important to you, getting your home sold for top dollar with a powerful Agent, or doing a good friend a favor?

Response J

You: I can understand that. Are you familiar with the techniques we use to get homes sold that other Agents were not able to get sold?

5. We're going to list with a new Agent.

Response A

You: Hey that's great! Have you already signed the contract with this Agent?
Seller: Yes.
You: Thank you for your time and have a great day! (Example of a condition)

Response B

You: Hey that's great! Have you already signed the contract with the other Agent?
Seller: Not yet.
You: OK, that sounds good. I would love to show you how I work. When would be the best time to show you?

Response C

You: Great, I would love to apply for the job. Are you familiar with the system I use to get my clients' homes sold faster and for more money than other Agents?
Seller: No.
You: That's exactly why we should get together. I found it's best for my clients to meet in the afternoon or evenings. Would 4 PM work or would 6 PM be better for your schedule?

6. We're going to take a break from the market/We're going to wait.

Response A

You: I can understand that. How long will you be taking a break?

(Whatever they say, ask if you can keep in touch from time to time. If they say yes, ask for their e-mail.)

You: Mr./Mrs. Seller, what's your email so I can send you my information about myself and how I work.

Response B

You: That makes sense. Your home was on the market for a minute. I feel your pain. What do you feel caused your home not to sell?

Response C

You: I can understand you want a break from the market. In the time your home was on the market, there were 35 homes that sold. If I was able to show you how our system can sell your home for top dollar would you want to hear more about it?

Response D

You: Mr./Mrs. Seller, are you still interested in selling at some point?

Seller: Yes, at some point.

You: This is all I'm proposing: before you decide to keep it off the market and possibly cost yourself tens of thousands of dollars, let me pop by and show you how I work differently than your last Agent. The meeting should only take 15 to 20 minutes to show you my proven system to get your property sold within 90 days. I'm available today at 2 PM or 5 PM or would tomorrow at 3 PM or 6 PM work for you?

7. How are you different from my last Agent?

Response A

You: What I am hearing you say is, how will I sell your home when your last Agent couldn't get the job done. Is this correct?

Seller: Yes.

You: It's a detailed process. I would like to pop by in the afternoon or evening to show you. Would 5 PM or 6 PM work best for you and your family?

Response B

You: Well, I am glad you asked. My office and I actually get homes **sold.** In the last 6 months while your home was on the market we **sold over 125 homes.** Would that be different?

Seller: Yes.

You: Do you want to know the good news, Mr./Mrs. Seller?

Seller: Yes.

You: We can do the same for you and your family. Wouldn't that be great?

Response C

You: You would like to know how I am different from your last Agent, I can understand that. You probably heard telling is not selling. So with your home's help, I can show you exactly why I'm different. This is all I'm proposing. When we can find the time to meet, I would like to go over three things with you:

First, I would like to pop by and show you exactly why your home did not sell. Second, I want to show you a few things that will definitely draw in qualified buyers interested in paying top dollar for your home. Mr. Seller, would you say that's pretty important for your bottom line?

Seller: Yes.

You: And the third thing is, I'm going to show you why my homes sell, and other Agents' homes do not sell in this marketplace. We can get together today at 5 PM or would 6:30 tomorrow be better for your schedule?

8. We changed our minds about selling/We're not selling!

Response A

You: You changed your mind about selling because you couldn't get it sold, or because you're just frustrated with the process?

Seller: (Agent wasn't able to get our home sold / yes, we're just sick of having it on the market)

You: Mr./Mrs. Seller, I completely understand some of the finest homes don't sell the first time. Before you make up your mind and keep your property off the market for any length of time, let me pop by to see your home. This way, I can quickly diagnose your home, and tell you exactly why your home did not sell. I can also show you some proven techniques that we use to get similar homes like yours sold in your area. What would be the best time to show you? Today at 5 PM or would 6:30 be better?

Response B

You: You changed your mind about selling, I can understand that. I'm just curious, at one point, you did want to sell...what changed?

Response C

You: I can understand where you are coming from. Selling or not selling is a business decision for you and your family. I'm just curious...if you can maximize the money that you could put in your pocket in the next 30 to 45 days would you want to hear more about it?

9. What's your commission?

Tip: Never ever talk about commission before the appointment. If you do, you will shoot yourself in the foot and regret it. Trust me, I know!

Response A
You: That's a great question. In the state of California (or your state) the commission is negotiable. That will be the first thing we will talk about when I see you.

Response B
You: Well it's free, and what I mean by that is, I don't charge you a dime unless I/we get your home sold for the price and the terms you agree to.

Response C
You: I'm willing to work for whatever we can agree to. That will depend on a few things, such as current market conditions, condition of the property, how much you want for the property, and how long you give me to sell it. I'm sure when we meet you'll be amazed at how I do business.

Response D
You: Mr./Mrs. Seller that's a great question. What I'm hearing you say is, you're really concerned about what you're going to net at the closing table. Am I right?

Response E
You: Mr./Mrs. Seller that will be the first thing we talk about when I see you. Our main goal is to use a proven system that will attract buyers that will pay top dollar for your home. Your goal is to make the most money for your home, isn't that right?

Response F
You: I can definitely understand your situation. I have several commission structures. Let's find a time when we can get together and work out the numbers, so

we can see if it will make sense for you and your family. I'm sure like most of my clients, you're not going to move forward unless the numbers make sense.

10. My last Agent said he'll cut his commission, will you?

These answers are for when you're at the appointment. If you sent them a pre-list package with a net sheet, you will not have to go through these objections. They will already know how much you charge.

Response A
You: I can understand that. Your last Agent cut his commission is that right?
Seller: Yes.
You: How did that work out for you?
Seller: Not good.
You: I definitely understand...everyone wants a deal. As you can see, cutting corners on the most expensive asset that you own is not financially productive correct?
Seller: Yes.
You: So, let's do this: list your property at a standard 6% Commission. That way, we can have all the buyer's Agents working extra hard to help us get your home sold at top dollar. Makes sense right?

Response B
You: Mr./Mrs. Seller, your last Agent cut his commission I see. Do you realize when an Agent cuts his commission, that affects your bottom line? Would you like to know why?
Seller: Sure.
You: Real estate is a commission-based business. In my opinion, this is extremely unethical. Did you know if an Agent looks at your listing in the MLS and see it is offering a discounted commission, that most Agents go right past it straight to your neighbor's home? You know, your competition down the street?

So let's do this: list your property at standard 6% commission. That way, we can get your property sold before your next neighbor closes escrow. Fair enough?

Response C
You: Your last Agent cut his commission, and you would like me to do the same correct?
Seller: Yes.

You: Usually a seller's home is their most valuable asset. Is this the case for you?

Seller: Yes.

You: I can understand that, and my job is to safeguard your equity and get you the most amount of money at the close of escrow correct?

Seller: Yes.

You: So let me ask you this quick question: if you were on an operating table about to have heart surgery, would you feel comfortable asking the doctor to give you a discount on the operation?

Seller: No.

You: So if a Real Estate Professional is willing to discount his commission just to receive your business, how would you know for sure he's doing his/her very best to safeguard the financial equity you worked so hard to build up?

Seller: Well, I don't know.

You: So, you won't have any doubts, let's list your property at standard 6% commission. Then you'll know that I'm doing everything I can to safeguard your equity and get your home sold for top dollar.

Response D

You: I see, your last Agent cut his commission and you would like me to do the same. Is that right?

Seller: Yes.

You: My Real Estate experience has taught me that if I did discount my commission, it is the equivalent of malpractice in the medical industry. I'll be doing you a grave disservice. No, I will not cut my commission. Any other questions?

Summary

Congratulations! For taking the steps necessary to complete this book. I'm proud of you. Not everyone can work expired listings successfully. In reading this book, you now understand it takes more than just learning scripts or objection handlers to be successful. You must have a thick skin, brass balls, the courage, and the strength the push through when needed.

Like we discussed earlier There's a lot of moving parts at play: the Agent and expired mindset. Knowing that part of the job when you're calling expireds is understanding the emotional turmoil they're going through.

You're like a doctor interviewing a patient to see exactly what's going on. As their professional, it's up to you to prescribe the right course of treatment.

Unfortunately, we can't help everyone. No matter what you say, or what script you use. You have come to realize by reading this book that it's a numbers game. It's going to be hard, difficult, and sometimes confusing.

You will push on and push through the difficulties. One day soon, you will have your Aha moment. And you will see a veil has been removed in front of you.

You will repeat your affirmation out loud every morning:

"I'm a Top Expired Listing Specialist and I help people! Who's next?"
"I'm a Top Expired Listing Specialist and I help people! Who's next?"

Now you can see your dreams turn into reality, the smell of success, and the feeling of victory. With all the hard work, determination, and focus, you now see yourself as a **Top Producer.**

Top 10 FSBO Objections

FOR SALE BY OWNERS ARE THE FASTEST SOURCE OF BUSINESS OPPORTUNITY!

Foreword

Man, I wish I had this book when I first started in real estate! I could have helped more people. I would have taken more listings... And made more money! Why? Because knowing **WHAT to say** to motivated prospects is half the battle. Yes, there are plenty of 'free' scripts and dialogs out there. But that's exactly the problem - using them will make you sound just like everybody else.

You already know that LISTINGS are the secret to success in this business. Easiest and often fastest listings are expireds and FSBOs.

When it comes to objections, most of the stuff taught these days by all those gurus and trainers is essentially arguing with the prospect. It's uncomfortable and ineffective. If anything, it's a safe road to piss good prospects off and lose a chance to help them.

This book is different because it's written by my student and friend **William May.** William is an active agent who -- just like you is in the trenches every day: working, prospecting, following up, hustling.

I've known William for over six or seven years. He's a graduate from one of the most intense real estate training programs in the world: The *"Double Your Listings Bootcamp".*
William is a rockstar real estate agent in an ultra-competitive market of Southern California.

The French say: *"Never trust a skinny chef!"* You want to learn the art of objection handling, then might as well learn it from someone who walks the walk just like you.

Getting this book was a smart choice. But it will only work if you implement it.

This is not a book to read. This is a workbook. A battle plan with answers to even the toughest FSBO objections.

Most agents don't work with FSBOs. Why? Mainly because they don't know what to say.

You're about to gain a huge advantage. This book will help you. Read it. Learn it. Practice it. Implement. Do it.

The best way to learn to ride a bike or any new skill for that matter is to stop overthinking it, get your butt up on the seat and just start pedaling. At first, it might feel a bit awkward and you might even fall down a couple of times before you get the hang of it, but before you know it you'll be riding like a pro.

Same thing here. Your confidence will come from experience. Practice this stuff daily and watch how quickly positive results - leads and listings - can follow.

FSBOs can be your 'bread-and-butter' listings. Just look around. The majority of them end up listing with a competent agent. And knowing what to say, how to answer sellers' questions and handle their objections can make you that agent - an FSBO Rockstar.

Best of luck on your journey!

Borino
Your Real Estate Coach

Borino is the author of the '*no resistance*' FSBO System for real estate agents **"The FSBORINO":** https://FSBORINO.com
Founder of one of the largest real estate groups for rockstar agents on Facebook: https://www.facebook.com/groups/rockstar.agents/

Introduction

You're driving down the street. You have your music playing in the background; it's a beautiful day with the sun shining and birds chirping, and suddenly off in the distance, you see a little sign. As it comes into focus you realize it is a FOR SALE BY OWNER sign. You become a little nervous. You start shaking, and a lump forms in your throat. You grip the steering wheel tighter as you slam on the gas to get away as quickly as you can.

In the back of your mind you know you should stop, pull over and go knock on that door! Yet you've been pre-programmed by other agents that FSBO sellers don't and won't respect you. They want to save the commission. Why should they hire you, when they could just sell their home themselves? And the excuses go on and on.

I'll be the first one to tell you that working with FSBO sellers is not for everyone, but every seller's situation is different. Let me ask you a quick question... How many people do you have to call, or doors do you have to knock on, to hit that ONE client who's looking to sell RIGHT NOW? Fifty, a hundred, maybe even a thousand?

We, as real estate agents, already know that it's a numbers game. I know this all too well, and that's why I love FSBO sellers! They're looking to sell NOW. So what if they want to try it on their own? You can't blame them for trying. If there were a way for you to save tens of thousands of dollars on any kind of sale, you would most likely do it yourself as well, wouldn't you? Of course, you would.

We are in the DIY generation. We all want to try and do everything ourselves, and if we find out we can't, then we'll just hire a professional to clean up our mess. Those are the for sale by owner sellers that I look for. That regular Joe who tried to sell his home on his own but couldn't. Now he's ready for a professional to step in and get the job done, and that's where we come in.

This book is going to teach you that working with for sale by owner sellers is a courtship. It's not a slam, bam, thank you ma'am kind of business. I'll teach you the FSBO mindset, and the best follow-up system. I'll teach you how to develop a relationship, over time, that will help to establish trust with your clients. I will also share with you my Top 10 For-Sale-By-Owner Objection Handlers so that you'll know how to communicate with the FSBO seller, answer their questions, and overcome their objections in a nice caring manner, that puts both sellers and agents at ease.

Nothing in this life is guaranteed, so I'll just promise you this... After reading this book, you will no longer think of FSBO's as scary, terrifying home sellers. You will learn, understand, and realize that from now on in your financial future, the abbreviation of F.S.B.O will stand for "The Fastest Source of Business Opportunity!"

So let's get started, ok?

Chapter 1: What Are Your Goals in Real Estate?

Before we get into the nitty-gritty details of working with FSBO sellers; knowing how to talk to them, reasoning with them, and overcoming their fears and objections, you must first have an understanding of what you are looking to get out of a career in real estate. What are YOUR goals and dreams?

Just so we're on the same page, I'm going to keep it real. The real estate business is one of the hardest businesses known to man. It's a selling game, and most people just do not know how to sell. You're not really selling real estate, you're selling yourself. You're demonstrating to your potential client that you can get their house sold fast, for top dollar, and with the least amount of hassle. That's what it all boils down to -- your confidence and your willingness to go the extra mile to take care of business.

No matter what type of goals you have in real estate, in order to be successful and support your family you must follow a successful plan of action. For example: have an exit strategy. You should work towards purchasing income property for yourself once every year or two so that when you retire from the real estate game, you'll have a passive income for years to come.

Another proactive way to be successful in real estate is to have a proven business model. Make a prospecting schedule, where you beat the pavement or make those cold calls. Have a lunch schedule that you stick to, so you may avoid too much downtime. Take time to study your real estate profession and learn your scripts and dialogs. That's digging in and getting to know your craft! Your hard work will pay off in the end.

You become what you focus on most of the time, so if you're focusing on being successful and learning your craft, eventually it will materialize.

Real estate is not a side gig. It is a full-time commitment. In the beginning, you might need to do it part-time as a means of supplemental income, and that's understandable. We all have to start somewhere. But every chance you get, you need to be studying, learning, and getting to know your chosen profession. Hard work, determination, and consistency are the fundamental keys to success. When you focus on the basics and you schedule your prospecting, it will become apparent that this is exactly how to make your dreams and goals come true.

SOLID GOLD TIP:

Prospect more than you think you should! Prospecting is the lifeblood of any successful real estate agent. If you do this it will definitely change your life for the better. Trust me.

Chapter 2: F.E.A.R.

F.E.A.R. There are many acronyms for the word fear. For example, False Evidence Appears Real; Forgetting Everything About Reality; Future Events Already Ruined. Is that little word "fear" holding you back from greatness? Let me tell you, each and every real estate agent that you know, and even the mega agents that you don't know, have had to face fear at some point in their career.

Fear is definitely something I'm familiar with. When I was in school, the teacher would call upon me to answer a question. It didn't matter if I knew the answer or not, I was simply scared to death. I just had anxiety during certain situations. And don't even mention public speaking! Getting up in front of people and have them stare at you, waiting to see what you're going to say. For most people, public speaking is their number one fear. It can be more frightening than spiders, snakes, dogs or germs. Public speaking will put most people into a panic. But when it comes down to it, fear is really a good thing.

Fear protects us and warns us that danger is lurking. When I was in elementary school, I was terrified of going to my new classroom on the second floor. It was in an older building, and the stairs were on the outside of the building. I was very young at the time, and I was deathly afraid of heights! There was literally nothing the teachers could say or do to get me up those stairs and into that room. They called my mother and let her know that they would reassign me to a class on the first floor. When my father got home, he was having no part of it. You have to understand, my father was a Marine, and he believed that you can be afraid, hell, you can even be terrified, but to be a true warrior you had to overcome those emotions. Push through the fear.

He gave me a time frame. The first month it was understood that I would go to the reassigned first-floor classroom, but every day I was to work on going up those stairs until I was able to get to the 2nd-floor classroom. All that my father asked of me was to conquer two stairs a day. Two steps, that's it. As a son looking to please his father, I accepted. My father would question me every evening when he got home from work. Had I honored our agreement? Did I make my steps? He kept me on track, and within a week and a half, I was in my new classroom. For the first month or two, I was still fearfully climbing those steps every day, but after a few months, my fear had all but disappeared.

The best way to get over your fears is to confront them head-on. If you're scared about cold calling, meeting people, working with FSBO sellers, or anything else, the best way to overcome your fears is by facing them every day. Here are a few tips to make prospecting FSBO's, or just prospecting in general, easier.

Tips to Prospecting with Less Stress and Fear

Know Your Scripts and Objection Handlers

There's a reason why you run across real estate coaches who have been successful in teaching top producing agents how to be the best in their profession. It's because they stress upon their students the importance of learning their scripts and objection handlers. Because knowing what to say, and how to say it, will eventually transform you into a better real estate agent communicator.

Knowing how to interact with whatever prospect you're dealing with will be a huge boost to your confidence. You will have less fear because you will know that whatever objection they throw at you, you can handle it. And you'll know in the worst-case scenario if you do not close your prospect, that doesn't make you a bad agent. You're here to help them, and if they're not in the position to receive your help, you have a clear understanding of their needs. That maybe this is not the right time for them, or this is not a client you wish to work with. Or if the chemistry isn't right, maybe it's just best to move on to the next prospect.

When you use scripts to talk to potential clients, it keeps the conversation flowing and on track. In this way, you can determine if the prospect is a potential client, or if they're just not interested right now. In other words, you're qualifying the prospect to see if they're in a position to sell and willing to work with you. Not to mention when you're using a good script you can double down and get to know the person and the situation that they're in more closely.

For example: What was their reason for moving into this particular neighborhood? What is the reason they're selling now? What do they like most about the neighborhood? How soon do they need to sell? How long will they try to sell on their own before they entertain other options?

Knowing, understanding, and implementing a good real estate script will excel your confidence, ignite your business, and put you ahead of your real estate competition. Real estate can be an easy business if you do not try to reinvent the wheel. Don't over-complicate things. Just follow the proven systems other successful real estate agents have used. All of them have some sort of script and objection handler they have used to be successful. They've done the research for you. You can simply use their tips and tricks to further your own success.

Know Your Business, Know Your Market Stats

One of the best ways to overcome fear and doubt, and boost your confidence in your real estate business, is to take your real estate business seriously. What do I mean by this? I mean by learning and knowing your trade. By following a set schedule every day to ensure success. By learning the contracts inside and out so you can best represent your client. Understand and know your local market stats in areas where you're prospecting. Know the average prices of homes sold in that area. Know the average days on market, average acreage, and the average square footage and the number of bathrooms. Knowing this information without hesitation when speaking to a client will definitely make you an authority in the prospect's mind.

If you're new in the business or in a sales slump, look into adopting a mentor to help you with your real estate business. Look for a top producing agent in your office or area that has integrity and a character that you highly respect. Invite that agent out for coffee or lunch. You'll be surprised how most successful agents are willing to share their secrets to success and their systems with you. In my experience, low producing agents are the ones that are more secretive about their success.

Your mentor does not have to be an agent in your office. Your mentor could be anyone, anywhere across the country, but I would suggest trying to get a mentor that's easily accessible, willing to work with you, and who knows your local market. Listen to that agent, and shadow that agent if possible.

Understand that an agent's time is valuable. They're taking time out of their busy schedule to invest in your future, so whatever advice they give you, pay attention! Take notes and understand that it's going to take some time to learn it, to tweak it, to adapt it to fit your needs, and to adopt it for your business. Be patient! Rome was not built in one day.

Prospect Every Day.

I'm not much of a reader, but since I began my career in real estate I have been introduced to many wonderful books on business and self-improvement. One of these books that I highly recommend is, "The Compound Effect", written by Darren

Hardy. One of the stories in the book, "The Story About the Penny", absolutely blew my mind.

(If you would like to see my suggestion of good real estate and motivational books, here is a link: williejmayenterprises.com/recommended-reads)

Let me ask you a question: If you could have $3 million right now, this second, in cold hard cash, or $0.01 that doubles every day for 31 days, which would you choose? Think about that for a second.

You might have heard this...... "For every day you prospect, it will pay you back sometime in the future. And for every day you do not prospect you will lose that opportunity forever". My broker continuously reminds me to "Build on my Successes". Once you have that real estate momentum going it becomes easier to get more business. That's why prospecting every day is so important. You build on each day's successes. You become used to your schedule. You have a need to prospect, to follow up, to make relationships happen. You'll see your efforts mature into closed transactions. Your daily prospecting is like The Compound Effect.

Which one did you choose? The $3 Million or the $0.01 that doubles every day for 31 days? With the power of The Compound Effect, did you know that after 31 days that single penny will transform into $10,737,418? When I first read that I couldn't believe it! I had to look it up, but incredibly the math works out.

- Day 1: $0.01
- Day 5: $1.00
- Day 10: $5.12
- Day 15: $163.84
- Day 18: $1,310.72

After day 18 you'll start to see how The Compound Effect begins really working its magic.

- Day 20: $5,242.88
- Day 25: $167,772.16
- Day 28: $1,342177.28 Can you believe it? On day #28 it hit over a Million!
- Day 30: $5,368,709.12 The 30th day, it's now over 5 Million Dollars!
- Day 31: The last day, The Compound Effect is fully in force. The penny has reached a whopping **$10,737,418.23!** Wow, that's amazing!

It's an incredible story, but the numbers do not lie. I cannot stress this enough, that if you get into a habit where you are prospecting daily, you can use The Compound Effect to your advantage. The more people you contact, the more people you adopt into your database. The more people that get to know you, like you, and trust you, the more people who will call on you when it's time to sell or refer you to a friend. This will be the foundation of your business.

The wonderful thing about prospecting is that it works for all types of clients. For sale by owners, expired listings, centers of influence, database, and follow-ups. Have you ever wondered why top-producing agents still have business when the market shifts? It's because of their dedication to prospecting. You can almost say, that if you prospect daily, you will have a recession-proof business.

Agent Mindset

Agent mindset. Let's think about that for a moment. How do you feel about for sale by owner sellers? When you think of an FSBO do you get excited? Anxious? That you just can't wait to get in front of them to show them your system for putting more money in their pocket? Your system for getting their home sold faster than they thought possible, so they can move on with their dreams? Or are you the complete opposite? Scared, frightened, or frustrated? Are you unclear on the proper way to help them sell their home? If they're able to sell their home without a real estate agent, obviously they'll make more money, right? It must be true. It makes sense on paper, and that's what you tell yourself. So whenever you see a for sale by owner seller, do you turn tail and run?

Or maybe all the old veteran real estate agents in your office brainwashed you into thinking for sale by owner sellers are hard to work with. That they don't have any money, and they don't appreciate the value of a real estate agent. Or that you just cannot sustain a profitable business working with FSBO sellers. They've told you to just stay away from them and work your center influence and wait for the phone to ring. Let me ask you something... how that's working out for you?

This chapter on F.E.A.R. is to help you change your mindset about for sale by owner sellers. At the beginning of this chapter, I shared a few acronyms of F.E.A.R. One of those acronyms was: False Evidence Appears Real.

This acronym perfectly describes most agents' emotions when it comes to dealing with for sale by owner sellers.

So here it is in a nutshell: My Top 5 Suggestions to Overcoming Fear in Working with FSBOs.

#1 Affirmations: Have you ever heard the expression, "Whether you think you can, or you think you can't... you're right". Success is all about believing in yourself and knowing that no matter how many times you fall down, you must get back up and dust yourself off. Tell yourself you're going to make it. One of the best things that helped me to believe in myself was doing daily affirmations. Say some in the morning over coffee, in the middle of the day, or just before you go to sleep at night, and eventually they'll sink in and become a part of who you are.

I suggest you go on the internet and look up some affirmations that will help you believe in yourself and give you the power to know that no matter what happens in your life or who you encounter, you're the man or woman in charge of your own life. Here is a link to a YouTube video of an affirmation that I find inspiring. I strongly advise you to use a headset when listening to this affirmation.

Multi-Million Top Producing Real Estate Professional - MOTIVATIONAL POWERFUL AFFIRMATIONS

#2 Study the Market: Be on top of your game, and study your market. Know what the average sale price is in your area. Know what types of homes are selling where you work. Colonial? Traditional? Spanish style? Be familiar with the home builders in your area, past and present. Learn the different styles of homes and floor plans each area builder produces and which are the most popular.

I know of one agent who took it a bit further, and for every property he sold, if the original owner was in possession of the floor plans which the builder gave them, he would purchase those plans from the owner. Wow. Talk about going the extra mile. Imagine showing up at an FSBO property and having the floor plan to their style of home. That will definitely set you apart.

Know your area better than any other real estate agent. The average sales price, the absorption rate, times and places of the neighborhood book club or HOA meetings. Go one step further and double down on the information. For example: know which days the trash company comes to pick up the trash and recyclables. What are the names of different schools in the area, and how do they compare to other schools in the state? (You can find this information at **greatschools.org**.) Being well-informed and up-to-date on the available information will allow your clients to have more faith and trust in your ability to do your job well.

Knowing the area that you work in will give you confidence when working with FSBO sellers or any client for that matter and will allow you to be prepared for any off-the-wall questions that may pop up.

#3 Be Consistent: That's right, be consistent. Being a successful real estate agent means putting in the work. Nights, weekends, whenever you have a spare moment, you need to put in the hours now so you can be on cruise control tomorrow. It's kind of like when you first started in real estate, or when you're recovering from a sales slump... you're like a rocketship on the pad just about to launch, but you need to make sure you're fueled up and ready when that timer counts down to zero. Make sure all systems are go before you take off!

Once you blast off it means putting in the work Monday mornings through Sunday nights; open houses on weekends; knocking on doors and making those cold calls. You're laying down the foundation of your success, and it is NOT going to happen overnight. Develop a schedule and reach out to potential clients consistently. Put it on your daily agenda, say from 8 to 11:30, that you're on the phone making those calls, and again in the afternoon if you have spare time. Always remember that slow and steady wins the race.

#4 Work on your Scripts and Dialogues: I know in the beginning I was scared to death talking to for sale by owner sellers because I did not know what to say. That's why you need to develop a dialogue and memorize it. Most of the time, people who are trying to sell their own homes have one main reason for it: To save money. It's basically their one main objection to hiring an agent. Once you understand that there are really very few reasons for FSBO objections, it will be easier to create a dialogue addressing these few issues, and you'll become more confident in your ability to talk to these potential clients and put their minds at ease. This will also make it easier for you to pick up that phone and dial that number and make that appointment.

Just about everyone these days has a Facebook account, so ask your friends for help, or you may have someone in your office that you can partner with to role-play and go over your scripts. The more you practice your dialogues with other people, the better you'll become at talking to for sale by owner sellers, or any potential client for that matter. It will also boost your self-esteem, and make your work more exciting, rewarding, and even fun!

#5 Get started.....NOW! That's right get started RIGHT NOW! Well, right after you finish this book or audible book at least. Then drop everything and get on those phones! Conquer your fears and those FSBO sellers. All joking aside, the main advantage of starting right now is that you're putting your real estate business FIRST and getting a jump on the competition.

You: "But William, I don't know exactly what to say. I'm scared of the phone. What if they say 'yes, I'm ready to sell, come over,' and I don't know what to do?"

Don't worry! I've been through this, and every other agent in the world has been through this, and we've all survived. You're not alone. Picking up that phone the first time may be one of the hardest things you ever have to do, but sooner or later you're going to have to do it if you want to be successful in this business. You bought this book, so it's obvious you're looking for help and information that will help you to succeed. But the secret to success that you're looking for is right inside yourself. You alone have the power to succeed in your own life and your own career. I am merely providing you the information and the tools and resources to help make that climb a little easier, but I can't do the work for you. I can put a million dollars in front of you, but unless you take it and spend it or invest it or burn it, it's not going to do you or anyone any good.

Unfortunately, failing is sometimes a part of real estate. It's an uphill climb, but each step takes you closer to your goal. You're going to make a lot of calls. And occasionally you're going to find FSBO sellers that aren't ready or willing to work with you. Sometimes they may not even like you or care to give you a chance, and some will just hang up on you. Unfortunately, that's just part of the game. Just keep in mind that you're reaching out to people who DO actually want to sell their home, so if you continue to follow-up with them and show them just how invaluable of an agent you are, then over time you WILL win them over. And eventually, you will see that working with for sale by owner sellers is not as hard and scary as other agents may have made it seem. Maybe it was just difficult for them because they didn't invest the time and effort into those potential clients that you're willing to invest in.

To make a long story short, it all basically comes down to consistency, hard work, and persistence. Just make sure that you make your calls every day, practice your scripts and dialogues, and research your sales area. Over time your skills will get better, your dialogue will become second nature, and before you know it all the fears that you once had about contacting for sale by owner sellers will be but a distant memory.

Chapter 3: Working with FSBO's Successfully

When you start working in real estate, or rather, when you actually make up your mind that you want to be SUCCESSFUL in real estate, you should pick a few prospecting niches to focus your time and effort on. In this way, when you're lead generating, you're maximizing your time to generate the best results.

FSBO leads are my favorite evergreen leads. Unlike other real estate markets that come and go at the drop of a hat, there is always a steady supply of For Sale By Owner Sellers! There may be one today, and five tomorrow. But one thing's for sure: no matter what your real estate market, FSBO leads will always be a consistent source of business.

Now with that said, you have to know how to work FSBO sellers because they're not your typical lead. I like to think of for sale by owner sellers as a fine wine. All good or exceptional wines must be aged appropriately for the maximum best taste when you drink it. In that same way, you must develop a relationship with these potential clients. Get to know them, give thoughts and ideas time to age, and let them breathe.

If the seller has a $300,000 home and you're being paid a 6% commission, that equals out to $18,000. That's a lot of money coming out of the seller's pocket. No matter what you say to the seller, it will fall on deaf ears unless they actually try the selling process on their own. Eventually, they're going to realize that it's not as easy as it seems. Always remember "Telling is not Selling". There is no better teacher than experience.

Never forget that working with For Sale By Owner sellers is a long game. You may have to follow up anywhere from 8 to 20 times in order to convert to a sale, and this may vary in different real estate markets.

Remember this when you're trying to work with an FSBO

- Give the seller time to get to know you.
- Give the seller time to get to like you.
- The seller needs to realize they can trust you.

No FSBO will work with you if they don't know you, like you, and/or trust you. The simplest, most effective way to work with For Sale By Owner Sellers is just to stay in contact with them once a week from the initial contact. **This is not rocket science; it's not brain surgery. It's so simplistic that I'm unsure why it's extremely hard for 90% of the agents out there to get it. They believe there has to be something more to it, but there isn't.**

I'm sure you've heard the saying.... "The money is in the follow-up." The main ingredient in working with For Sale By Owner Sellers is **Your Follow-Up!**

FSBO Mindset

An additional key to working with for sale by owner sellers is that you have to understand their mindset, and their typical mindset is: "I want to sell my property on my own so I can save as much money as possible". I stated this in my introduction into this book, and that we are living in a Do-It-Yourself day and age, where people feel like they can and should handle all aspects of their lives themselves.

I'm not sure about you, but if there's a way for me to save tens of thousands of dollars by doing something myself, then I'm all for it. But what FSBO sellers don't realize is that saving that money by not paying a commission may look good on paper, but they're actually losing more than they think.

And that's our job, isn't it? To be an asset to our potential clients and help them with the things they do NOT realize.

There are basically THREE types of FSBO sellers:

#1 The Newbie:
They believe that selling real estate is easy, no problem, and anyone can do it! For Sale sign in the yard? Check! Ad in the local paper? Check! Craigslist ad? Check! Schedule an open house this weekend? Check! They're so excited, yet so naive, that they think once they hold that open house, potential buyers will just show up with bags and bags of cash.

#2 The Seasoned Seller:
These sellers have been in the game for a while. They can see a real estate agent coming from a mile away. They are an "expert" when talking to agents, and they have their own scripts and dialogues memorized. "Can you bring me a buyer?

What's your commission? Will you take 2%? Another agent said they would". And the list of objections goes on and on.

(The answer to that 2% objection is "No, Sir. Let me ask you, how many weeks out of the year do you work for your boss for free? If we decide to work together, I'm sure we can negotiate a commission that is fair to both of us and still allows the house to sell. I would love to take a look at your home. Would today at 5:00 work, or would 6:30 be better?")

#3 The Burnt-Out Seller:
The fast cash and easy sale of his home that he imagined, in the beginning, has become a distant memory. This seller no longer answers his phone calls but screens them. He no longer listens to voicemails, but deletes them a whole batch at a time, because he or she has come to the realization that the only people calling about their property are more real estate agents wanting to take the listing. This for sale by owner seller is on the brink of throwing in the towel.

The burnt-out seller is just frustrated, and expectedly so. With a little practice rehearsing your scripts and some on-the-job training calling FSBO sellers, you'll have a higher probability of converting them in stages 2 and 3 of this example. The key is a consistent follow-up. If you've been contacting them since they listed their home, or close to it, and you've been contacting them once or twice a week since then, you've been building a rapport with them, and are better able to answer their questions. Maybe you even had the opportunity to stop by during their open house, or you were able to set an appointment to preview the property. All of this hard work and dedication adds up to a potential listing.

I want to be clear here, I am not guaranteeing you any type of results. Your results will vary from state to state, market to market, seller to seller. Nothing in this life is guaranteed, as we all know. But you can't succeed if you don't work the system. All you need to do is pick up the phone every day and make your calls, and don't ever give up. And if you follow these examples of hard work, dedication, and consistency, then there's NO reason why you wouldn't or can't succeed.

Chapter 4: Frequently Asked Questions

Where do I get the numbers?

There are several different services to get FSBO numbers or numbers in general in the real estate business. There are not as many landlines as there were back in the day, but there ARE websites.

I've tried several different FSBO services. In my opinion, you should try various services and find out which ones work best for you and your market.

FSBO services: (In no particular order)

1. Zillow.com
2. Trulia.com
3. Red X
4. Land Voice
5. Vulcan7
6. Rebo Gateway
7. Mojo Sells-Lead store (I personally use and endorse)
8. Espressoagnt.com
9. Forsalebyowner.com
10. Fizber.com
11. 4salebyowner.com
12. Fsbo.com
13. Fsbo-home.com
14. Hotpads.com
15. byownerdaily.com

And the list goes on and on. When you're prospecting FSBO sellers, understand that they're a different beast. You may have to cold-call hundreds, even thousands of numbers to get in touch with someone who may be thinking about selling their home sometime in the near future.

But on the other hand, when you are calling FSBOs, they're hot, they're ready, and they want to sell NOW! How many cold calls do you have to make before you run into a client who's looking to sell? How many doors do you have to knock? How many people in your database do you have to call? How many expired listings do you have to check on or show up to, to finally get that listing? As many as it takes. When you finally find that FSBO seller, they're looking to sell RIGHT NOW. The only catch is they wanted to do it on their own. No problem! The hard part is already done: the searching, finding, and identifying a homeowner who's looking to sell. Now all you have to do is convince them that you should help them!

When it comes to selling real estate, the slogan I use in my advertising is **"GET SOLD NOW"**. Out of all the leads out there other than the **COME LIST ME LEADS,** FSBOs are probably one of the best sources of ripe, low-hanging fruit listing businesses out there. Are you ready to harvest your success?

What is the best CRM to use?

So how do you decide which is the best Customer Relationship Management System (CRM) to use? Fellow real estate agents have been asking that question since the beginning of time. There are so many different kinds of CRM's out there that you're bound to find one that fits your needs. Some are more advanced than others, and some are super simplistic.

If you're a new agent, and you've found a simple, easy-to-use system to retrieve your data, then use it. Stick with it, and when you get to a certain level where you've mastered that system and want something more challenging or more powerful, that's when it's time to start experimenting with other, more advanced contact management systems.

If you're an agent that's been in the game for a while and you're tired of your current CRM, then experiment with other systems that are available. Usually, they'll offer a free trial or some sort of promotion to get your precious business. Change it up, and keep it fresh!

Need a few examples? How about Top Producer, Red X, Mojo Dialer, Infusionsoft, Salesforce, BoomTown, and the list goes on and on. You get the picture.

Well, William, you may ask, what CRM do you use? I actually use two CRM's. Yes, I'm crazy like that. The truth is, for right now it's best for me to use two systems in my business, but eventually, that may change. Like I mentioned earlier, you have to treat your business like a living, growing business. When it grows, you must grow with it.

I use the Mojo Dialer and Contactually. I have to give Mojo Dialer credit. In the last few years, they have developed into a very powerful CRM with a 3-line dialer.

I'm not going to go into detail. I primarily use Mojo for the dialing system to circle prospect: Cold calling, Expired, For Sale By Owners & My People Farm.

Contactually is the second CRM that I use. I enjoy their simple interface and ease-of-use. I primarily use Contactually for working my Spear of Influence (SOI), and my database. Unfortunately, Contactually doesn't have a dialing system, but I don't hold that against them.

Just take your time and do your own due diligence. See which program best fits you, your business and your personality.

What is the best auto dialer to use?

You have Turbodial for Infusionsoft, Vulkan 7, Redx Storm Dialer, and quite a few others. The whole purpose of using an autodialer is to be more efficient in your prospecting. There are many types of auto-dialers. Some have a single line, and some have a multi-line set up.

If you're a new agent or just starting out calling For Sale By Owner sellers, I would suggest you start with the old-fashioned method. Use your cell phone, office phone, or your home phone. These are high-quality leads you do not want to lose because of a bad connection or a delayed connection.

When you're new at calling FSBO sellers, it's best to get comfortable with calling them one at a time. Do not rush it, just take your time. If you work with them in this way, your comfort level and experience in dealing with these sellers will increase. Only then would I suggest moving to an autodialer.

My auto-dialer of choice is the Mojo sales dialer. I can cold call and/or circle prospect with their 3-line dialer. The system can call up to 300 numbers per hour. It's a tremendous time-saver over calling one at a time on your own phone. And as an added bonus, if I don't have that many numbers to call I can adjust the dialing system to 2 lines or 1. And just recently they added a new service called "Click-to-Call". Click-to-call gives you all the time you need to review the information before you click that button, and then it auto dials the client. (Thanks, Mojo, for adding that great feature!)

Another bonus in the Mojo system is that you can set up groups. I have divided For Sale By Owner Sellers into two groups: New For Sale By Owners, and Old For Sale By Owners. These groups helped me stay organized and on point when I'm prospecting my potential FSBO clients.

Should I Leave a Message?

When calling for sale by owner sellers, it is always good to leave a voicemail. Just make sure your voicemail is to the point, short and sweet.

Example: "Hello, my name is William May, and I'm a real estate agent with Happy-Go-Lucky Real Estate. I see that your home is for sale by owner. Congratulations! I've seen your ad, and I have a few questions regarding your home. As I'm sure you know, most homes like yours sell quickly. Is your home still available? If so, would it be available for viewing if I have any buyers that are interested in your particular home? You can contact me at 323-123-4567. Thank you for your time and have a great day!"

As you can see this message is short, polite, and to the point, and identified a few key subjects. First, I identify myself as a real estate agent. Second, I let them know that I'm aware that the home is for sale by the owner of the property, and also showing some enthusiasm by saying congratulations! This lowers their guard a little bit, so I don't just seem like another agent wanting to take their listing.

Thirdly, I'm letting the homeowner know the reasons for my call: that I have a few questions regarding the property. They become curious because they already know that I've seen their ad since I told them I did, so the most common questions should already be answered. (That is if the ad was written correctly.) So, this piques their curiosity and gives them a reason to speak with me.

In my experience, when I first started cold calling without a dialer, leaving messages took a lot of my time. But I received 2 great listings from cold calling, and one I was able to double end. So, leave messages like you're playing the lottery, because you can't win unless you play!

Should I Tell the FSBO Seller That I Have a Buyer When I Really Don't?

Absolutely not! You do remember your code of ethics, correct? If you want to be successful in this business, you always need to be upfront and honest. Yes, sometimes that may hurt your pocketbook. As for myself, I'm not going to sell my soul to the devil for a commission check. People are selling the most expensive and valuable asset in their lives. They need to work with an agent who is honest and trustworthy and is always looking out for their best interest. Always keep your integrity intact. Your reputation depends on it.

Chapter 5: Do You Have The Drive And Determination to Succeed?

Do you think you have what it takes to succeed in this crazy, mixed-up world of real estate? As of 2018, the real estate industry is ranked 12th in agent turnovers. Mainly because most real estate agents entering the business are not fully prepared for the reality of the real estate market. They are so used to working nine-to-five jobs and having a boss looking over their shoulder to make sure they stay on track and do what they need to do. But once they enter into real estate there is no accountability. You have to look over your own shoulder and keep yourself on track.

In most brokerages, they give you a cubicle, The Haines directory, and tell you.... "Good luck, make those calls!" Then they throw you in the deep end, and it's sink or swim. If you learn to swim, great! You make yourself, your family, and their broker money, and all is good in the world. But if you don't, you drown, and eventually, become a distant memory. The good news is, it doesn't have to be that way! Real estate can be an easy, fun, and wonderful business to grow in. But it takes commitment, learning, and... oh yes, a whole lot of hard work. Remember, nothing worth having comes easy, and nothing that comes easy is worth having. Here are a few tips to help your drive and determination kick in for success.

Consistency
You can do open houses, door-knocking, and phone prospecting. The best thing you can do is to get face-to-face, belly-to-belly, with as many potential customers as you can. And once you have a steady flow of income, then you can take the weekends off to spend more time with your family. And believe me.... that's priceless!

It's a Numbers Game!
Did you know that the numbers are in your favor? Did you know that homeowners are **70% more likely to use the first agent that they come in contact with?** It sounds like good news to me!

I don't understand a lot of these coaches and trainers who throw out these ridiculous numbers like, "For every 10 FSBO you call, you'll get one listing" or something ridiculous like that. I believe in real-world numbers, and it's not that pretty or that easy. Being successful, like I say, is hard work.

These numbers are just an example of the worst-case scenario. As you know, your results may vary, but once you start the process and get more familiar with your prospecting style and contact ratio, the numbers will develop a pattern that you can use to build your successful business.

For example, let's say you have to dial 100 numbers to get 2 contacts.
And let's say you need 100 contacts to generate 2 good leads.
And let's say you need 50 good leads to generate 1 appointment.
And let's say you need to make three appointments to take just one listing.

See how the number game works? If you're not fortunate enough to be like some of these uber-successful real estate agents who seem to have an armored truck full of cash to pay for marketing, mailers, and retargeting ads to retrieve their business, then you're just going to have to prospect. To hustle like any other hungry real estate agent that wants to succeed.

The hardcore truth is, you need to first focus on the basics: Coming into the office early every morning, practicing your scripts, role-playing with other agents, and you stay on that phone all day long if you have to. Eventually, you'll become a master at telephone prospecting. And then you move on to door knocking, open houses, or whatever form of prospecting you feel comfortable with. Master it, and be consistent with it, and eventually, you WILL be a success.

Chapter 6: Tools You Will Need

Your Calendar

Either a physical calendar, or a digital calendar, or both. The calendar is one of the main tools for being successful in real estate. Become accustomed to scheduling everything in your calendar. Spending time with the family, doctor and dentist appointments, your family vacations. Anything and everything must go into the calendar so that you can stay on track with your business and know when you can be available to potential clients.

Make sure most importantly that you schedule your prospecting as a recurring appointment. And do NOT schedule your listing appointments during prospecting hours. The only exception to the rule is if you're new or you're in a sales slump. Then, of course, drop everything and get that listing!

Workstation

You'll need a quiet and distraction-free work environment. This could be anywhere in your home or work office. Just anywhere you can be productive without distractions.

Computer or Laptop

In this tech-savvy world, I don't see how it's even possible to have a real estate business without a computer. The computer or laptop doesn't have to be state-of-the-art or have all the bells and whistles known to man. Just as long as you have a digital device that will help you prospect. I mainly work off of my home PC. At the office, I use my laptop simply because it's very mobile and convenient if I have to pick up and go to a conference room or to a meeting in another agent's office.

I also use an iPad on the go. This is very convenient for me for several reasons. I could use it at a meeting, or at a business lunch, or for general prospecting on-the-go, which allows me to log into my Mojo dialing system or into my CRM. I also take it with me on listing presentations, just in case I need to show clients a detail about comparable sales in the area.

Telephone

It is a must to have a good reliable smartphone. It doesn't matter if it's Apple, Samsung, Motorola or a BlackBerry. As long as you have a phone that is dependable, with good service and a good data plan, so you can conduct your business in a professional manner.

Your Car

I want you to understand this, you don't need a $100,000 BMW to be successful in real estate. Make do with what you have, and upgrade if necessary once the means become available. However, it is imperative that you have dependable transportation.

Chapter 7: FSBO Objections

There is definitely a system to the madness. No matter what script you decide to use, your end goal is the same: to generate appointments, to determine if a lead is worth following up, or if the lead is trash. The reflex answer to objections is usually no, so in the first part of the conversation most of the time you can just shelve that objection. If it is serious enough the client will bring it back up later in the conversation, and that's where you have to make a decision on the best way to handle that objection.

Always repeat, affirm, and then ask another question. Mirror and match the client. Let the potential client speak 80% of the time, and you only 20% of the time, mostly with questions. Statistics have shown that the more someone talks and asks questions, the more rapport you build. Focus on their needs that wants but keep the endgame in mind. Knowing your scripts and dialogues is not enough. You must practice them. The more prospecting that you do, the better you will be with your communication.

Top 10 Objections

#1 I Only Work with Buyer's Agents.

#2 I Can Sell the House on My Own, I've Done it Before.

#3 I Cannot Afford to Pay Your Commission.

#4 Will You Cut Your Commission?

#5 I Will Use a Discount Broker and List It on the MLS.

#6 We Already Have an Agent We Will Use if We Can't Sell on Our Own.

#7 We Will Use Our Family Member Who is an Agent.

 # 8 Do You Have a Buyer?

#9 Bring Me a Buyer and I Will Pay 3%.

#10 What Are YOU Going to do Differently to Sell My Home?

#11 Bonus Objection: What's Your Commission?

Chapter 8: Top 10 FSBO Objections

1. I Only Work with Buyer's Agents.

A) OK great, now let me make sure I have this correct... You're only willing to work with buyer's agents, correct? **(Yes.)** Is that agent working for you or the buyer? **(The buyer.)** So, if you take a second to think about it, the buyer's agent is not looking out for your best interests, only the buyers' best interests, correct? **(Yes.)** So how about this: Let's make an appointment for me to come over and see your home. This way we can discuss some options on selling your home for the most money, and make sure that we have YOUR best interests at heart. Does this make sense? **(Yes.)** Fabulous! I'll be in your area around 3 today or would 4 be better for your schedule?

B) Wow, only with buyer's agents? May I ask, how you feel that will help your bottom line?

(Notice how I acknowledged what they said, then immediately I intentionally asked another question. This is what you call "Shelving That Objection". It's like a reflex NO. Another point to remember is that he/she that asks questions maintains control of the conversation.)

C) OK, great. You only work with buyers agents. I can understand that, but let me ask you a quick question... I have plenty of experience helping people such as yourself to sell their homes and have the buyers fight over the privilege of purchasing them. If I can show you a proven system where your home will not sit on the market but will sell quickly for top market value, would you at least want to hear about it?

(If they say yes, set an appointment. If they say no, which in most cases they will, but not all the time, send them a thank-you card and follow up once a week until they say... stop contacting me! Or until they list with another agent. Remember that working with FSBO sellers is a matter of rapport and familiarity. They have to understand and believe your continuous communication is in their best interest. Once they realize that it is, along with getting to know you, they will list with you. Why? Because you have earned their trust.)

2. I Can Sell the House on My Own, I've Done it Before.

A) Hey, that's great! I sell homes all day, every day as well. Like my father used to say, "If you love your what you do, you'll never have to work a day in your life." (Shelf the objection and move on) So when this home sells, where are you moving to?

B) Congratulations! I don't have to tell you that selling a property is not as easy as it looks. I/We, this year alone, sold over 25 homes. Our success comes partly from our networking with Top Buyers Agents, my/our marketing plan, and my skills as a negotiator. Let me ask you if I can show you a proven plan to sell your home for top dollar, do all the work for you, and make this the smoothest transaction possible, would you want to hear more about it?

(If your production is not that high, just use your company stats as your market stats)

C) Hey, that's wonderful. What all are you doing to market your home? (Shelved objection and keep asking questions.)

3. I Cannot Afford Your Commission.

A) I understand exactly where you're coming from. Most FSBO sellers believe that at first, so they try to sell on their own, believing they can make more money that way. Unfortunately, they eventually come to the realization that it is not as easy as it looks, and in the meantime, they have wasted their valuable time, money, and effort.

I'm just curious, if you're able to put some real money in your pocket, are you serious about selling your home? **(Yes.)** Okay. I'm not in the habit of wasting anyone's time, yours or mine, so let me suggest this: I'll do my homework on your property and the market. I'll give you a call back and let you know all the information I recovered, and then we'll see if we can go to the next step. And if not, no harm, no foul. I'll keep in touch with you and be a resource for you and your family until the time is right. What do you say?

(When you get this objection sometimes it can be tricky because they may not have enough equity to sell, and if that's the case it is no longer an objection but is now a condition. A condition is something you cannot overcome at that specific time. But as is in this example, if they're low on equity that can change if/when the property value rises.)

B) I completely agree with you that selling your house using an agent such as myself is definitely a sizeable investment. But on the other hand, if I can show you with my proven system that I can sell your home for top dollar, and have it more than cover the cost of my commission, would you want to hear more about it?

C) I'm not one to argue, you have a valid point. Quick question: If there was a way, I could show you that I can sell your home for top market value and net you enough money to move forward with your family's plans, would you like to hear more about it? **(Yes.)** Great! I could pop by today at 5:00, or does 6:30 work better for your schedule?

(Always understand it doesn't matter what they tell you... I cannot afford to pay your commission, I don't want to pay any commission at all, your rates are too high, etc. Most of the time when they say these types of things, they are the same statements that they used to get rid of the last agent, so you have to ask questions to find out exactly where they stand. Set yourself apart from past agents. Ask questions and get to know their particular situation. It may be the case that they simply cannot pay your commission. That would be a condition, not an objection. Sometimes you just have to let a lead go and move on to the next. It's the nature of the business.)

4. Will You Cut Your Commission?

A) Commissions in the state of California are completely negotiable. Are you familiar with how commissions work in relation to selling your home? **(No.)** Okay, let's kill two birds with one stone. Let me pop by, take a look at your house, and I can answer any questions you may have regarding a commission or anything related to selling your house in this real estate market.

(When it comes to answering questions about the commission, it can be a very touchy subject. You're not going to win a listing by simply answering their questions over the phone. Always remember to acknowledge their question, immediately ask another question, or shelve the objection. Keep the conversation moving towards your ultimate goal, which is setting an appointment.)

B) That's a great question. I'm willing to work for whatever price we can agree to. Let me ask you, when you sell this home, where is your family moving to next?
(Keep the conversation moving by answering and immediately asking another question.)

C) Let me ask you a question: How many weeks out of the year do you work for your boss for free?

(Wait for their response. And remember, the first person that speaks, loses.)

I'm a very aggressive agent when it comes to working with my clients. Part of my job as your agent is being a good negotiator. If I cannot negotiate my commission with you, how would I be able to negotiate the best price for your home with a potential buyer?

Offer to set up a time when you can take a look at their home. Include things like, "Once I see what type of property I'm working with, we can discuss a commission that works best for you, for me, and still allows the home to sell for top dollar. Fair enough?"

D) I'm willing to work for whatever amount we can agree to, and that will depend on a few things, such as.... current market conditions, condition of the property, the asking price for the property, and how long you give me to sell it. I'm sure when we meet, you will be very impressed with how I do business.

I like to meet people in the afternoons or evenings. Just be sure to ask what day and time of day would work best for them.

(In my opinion, the commission objection is the most difficult objection for agents to handle. If you make time in your schedule to practice role-playing and rehearse with other agents, this or any other objection should no longer be an issue for you.)

5. I Will Use a Discount Broker and List it on the MLS.

A) So you want to use a discount broker and put it on the MLS, is that correct? **(Yes.)** I'm just curious, in your opinion, how does this strategy help you and your family get your property sold? (Basically, they'll tell you it's by saving the commission or something of that nature.)

Okay, I see, and I can understand your point. It looks good on paper. But what if I could show you a way that I could save you time, money and effort, and most importantly SELL your house quickly, all the while putting the MOST money in your pocket? If that was possible, you would definitely be open to hearing more about that, wouldn't you? (How could they not say yes?)

B) Am I hearing you correctly,. discount broker? **(Yes.)** May I ask, what will he or she do differently than myself to get your home sold? (Basically, they won't know how to answer this question. The only thing they may say is: the commission is cheaper / there is a cheap flat fee / the agency will list it on the MLS, or something to that effect.)

To which you reply, "I see. Have they provided you with a written guarantee that they will not charge you a dime unless your home sells?" **(No.)** Then let's do this, I don't mind... I can pop over today and show you my proven system that has helped many of my clients get their home sold quickly for top dollar, and with this system, you'll see that I don't charge you anything until your home is sold.

Would you be available today at 5 or would 6:30 be better for your schedule? (This forces them to choose a time for that appointment.)

Be sure to get their email address so you can send them more information about yourself and your sales system and share your contact information with them as well.

C) In my experience, most of my clients use a discount broker because they're looking to save the most money. Is that the case for you? **(Yes.)**

That makes sense to me. Let me just send you my marketing plan so that way you can compare my proven system to their marketing plan. In this way, you can make an educated decision on which company is going to net you the most amount of money.

You are looking to put the most money in your pocket when you sell your home, aren't you? **(Yes I am, but they have not provided me with any kind of marketing plan.)** Wow, they haven't? I know most companies just charge a flat fee, post your property on MLS, and basically tell you to sit back for a couple of months until your home sells for a discounted price.

This is called **Post and Pray.** Are you looking to sell your property for a discounted price? **(Hell no!)** Then how about I send you my proven marketing plan so that you can see exactly how I get my clients' homes sold for top dollar? What's your email address? **(Hot-home-seller@gmail.com)** Okay great. I'm available this evening between 5:00 and 7:00. What time would be best for you?

Valuable Tip: This extra step works wonders: After you set the appointment and email them your pre-listing package or your marketing plan, have a messenger or courier service deliver your package. Make sure it arrives before the scheduled appointment. Ideally, you want to have it delivered within 2 hours of speaking to them.

When you're dealing with listings out here in Southern California where prices are $400,000 and up, you get up out of your chair and deliver the package yourself. I have even paid an Uber driver many times to deliver my pre-list package. These special touches will put you head and shoulders above your competition.

I am currently working on the course that teaches you how to make your own Pre-List Package & Marketing Plan. If you're interested, please email me at Williejaymay@gmail.com

6. We Already Have an Agent We Will Use If We Can't Sell On Our Own.

A) Okay, I can understand that you're going to use someone that you already have in mind. (I am shelving that objection) How long will you be trying to sell your property on your own before you decide to use an agent? **(Maybe 2 weeks.)** Hey, that's great.

Are you willing to work with agents that can bring you a buyer? **(Yes, we will pay 3%.)** You will pay 3% to a buyer's agent, that makes sense. Our office has over a hundred and fifty agents. On average each of our agents is usually working with two or three buyers at a time. I would love to stop by your property to take a look at it. This way we can meet in person and I can see what type of home you have to offer to potential buyers.

I like to meet with people in the early afternoons or on weekends. I can pop by today at 5 or would Saturday at 2 work best for your schedule?

B) I completely understand. I've been in the real estate game for a while now, and almost everyone has at least one person in their family or circle of friends that is an agent or knows an agent.

Quick question... if I had a buyer who's willing to pay full price for your home, and is in the position to close within 30 to 45 days, would that be of some interest to you? **(Sounds great, but do you actually have a buyer?)**

Possibly, but I don't know because I haven't seen your house yet. I'll be in your neighborhood today between 4:30/5:00. How about I stop by and take a look at your home, so I can see exactly what you have to offer for today's buyers. I can also show you exactly how I get homes sold for top market value with my marketing plan, proven to attract buyers who are looking for properties just like yours. So would 5:00 work for you? I'd love to show you how I can get your home sold in the next 30 to 45 days.

7. We Will Use Our Family Member Who Is an Agent.

I can almost anticipate what's going through your mind right now as you read that objection. 90% of real estate agents hear this objection and hang up the phone right away. That's understandable because 80% of the time when you hear this objection is not really an objection. **It's a condition.** And the only way to find out if it's a condition or an objection is to make the call and have a conversation.

A) That's wonderful. It's always good to know someone in the business. I sell a lot of homes in the area, maybe I have worked with them in the past. What is their name? (**Well, they do not really work in the area.**)Ok, I have an idea. How about I pop by and take a look at your home, and show you how I sell my clients' homes for the most money, and if the numbers make sense to you maybe we can work out a referral for your family members? It's a win-win for everyone. I can pop by today at 5:00, or would 6:30 be better for your schedule?

B) That's great. It's always good to know someone in the business. I sell a lot of homes in the area, maybe I have worked with them in the past. What is their name? (**James Calhoun, of ABC Realty right here in town. Have you heard of him?**) No, I haven't heard of him, but I'm sure he's an excellent agent. Have you signed a listing contract yet? (**No, not yet.**)

In my experience, it's always good to have two companies competing for your business, so you can determine which company best fits your needs and expectations. I highly respect that you're considering a family member, but keep in mind we are dealing with the most expensive asset most people own in their lifetime. How about I just send you my marketing plan, and my proven system on how I sell homes and get top dollar for my clients? This way you can compare my marketing plan with James', and you can make an educated decision on which agent is the best fit to sell your home. Make sense?

They can either say, "Yes, send me over your information", or they can say "No thanks, I'm just not interested". When they say no, simply reply with.... "It's been a pleasure speaking with you. If anything changes, please don't hesitate to call. Have a great day!" You might ask me, "William, with a conversation like this, after they've shut you down, would you still send them a thank you card?" The answer is always YES. No matter who you talk to, always take the time to send them a thank-you card. You never know what may happen in the future. I have had clients who sold their home with another agent, but because I sent them that thank you card, they sent me a referral. Real estate is funny that way, and that's why I love it.

C) That's great. It's always good to know someone in the business. I sell a lot of homes in the area, maybe I have worked with them in the past. What is their name? (**None of your business/you don't need to know. Do you have a buyer?**) I don't know, maybe. I haven't seen the house yet. If I did have a buyer, are you willing to cooperate with buyers agents? **(Yes, but I'm only paying 2% and not a penny more!)** Hey, that's great. Good luck and thank you for your time. Have a great day!

(Sometimes, inevitably, you'll run into people that have an attitude. Do not take this personally, it's just part of the job. They're not upset with you. Maybe they are upset because they're only receiving calls from agents and not buyers. Maybe they're just having a bad day. Or maybe there has been a death in their family, and they're carrying the burden of trying to sell the house and handle the estate. Maybe they've lost their job and are being forced to sell a home that they love. All of these things can be extremely stressful, so when you're prospecting and calling FSBO sellers, keep an open mind, and always be compassionate to the people you speak to.)

8. Do You Have a Buyer?

A) Possibly. Our office has over 50 agents that work with an average of 3 buyers each. If we can generate a full price offer and get you sold and moved on with your life, that would definitely work for you and your family......right?

B) Let me ask you, what type of buyer are you looking for? (No matter what they say, reply with the following.) Ok, we can both agree that the best buyer is someone who is ready and willing to pay your price and that can close escrow, correct? If I/we can generate that buyer and get you back on track with your original plans, are you ready to put me/us to work?

C) You know what, that's a good question. I can't answer right now, because I haven't even seen your house yet. Are you still interested in selling? (Continue with the script and set that appointment when appropriate.)

9. Bring Me a Buyer and I Will Pay 3%.

A) Okay, great! If I bring you a buyer, you're willing to pay a 3% commission, is this correct? **(Yes.)** Then it seems to me that we're on the same page. When would be a good time for me to come by and take a look at your home, so that I may show you exactly how I get my clients' homes sold for top dollar? I'll be in the neighborhood later on today. When would be the best time to pop by? This afternoon at 4:00, or would 5:30 be best for you?

B) A 3% commission, that's excellent. I'll make a note of that. By the way, you have a wonderful home. Would you happen to know how old the roof is? (Shelve the objection and continue on with your script, and when the time is right, close for the appointment.)

C) That's fantastic! Our office has over a hundred and fifty agents, and on average each agent is working with two or three buyers at a time, so I'm sure we can get your home sold. From what you've told me so far, it sounds like you have a wonderful home. When would be the best time for me to stop by and see it for myself? So that I can have an accurate idea of what you're offering the real estate market for today's buyers.

Work out an appointment time that works best for your seller and yourself and get down to business!

10. What Are You Going to do Differently to Sell My Home?

A) What am hearing you say is, how will I sell your home for top dollar? Is this correct? **(Yes.)** Well, it is a detailed process. I would like to stop by this afternoon or evening to explain it to you. What time would work best for you and your family?

B) Well, I am glad you asked. My office and I actually get homes **SOLD.** In the last 6 months or so, while your home was on the FSBO market, we **SOLD over 125 homes!** Would that be different? **(Yes.)** And do you know what the good news is, Mr/Mrs. Seller? We can do the same for you and your family! Wouldn't that be great?

C) You would like to know how I am different, and I can understand that. You've probably heard the saying, "telling is not selling". If you'll set a time for me to explain my plan for selling your home, I'll show you how I am different.

When we meet, I would like to go over three things with you:

First, I would like to stop by to view your home and show you exactly why your home did not sell.

Second, I would like to show you a few things that will definitely draw in qualified buyers interested in paying top dollar for your home. Mr. Seller, would you say that's pretty important for your bottom line? **(Yes.)**

The third thing I would like to show you is how we get results, while other FSBO homes do not sell for top dollar in this marketplace. My system and results show that I get homes sold for top market value. Can we get together today at 5 PM, or would 6:30 tomorrow be better for your schedule? I will have my results ready for you.

Bonus Objection: What Is Your Commission?

Tip: Never ever talk about commission before the appointment. If you do, you will lose whatever chance you have setting that appointment and getting the listing. **Trust me on this!**

A) That's a great question. In the state of California, (or your state), the commission is negotiable, and that will be the first thing we will talk about when I see you.

B) Well, for now, it's free! What I mean by that is, I won't charge you a dime unless I/we get your home sold for the price and the terms you agreed to.

C) I am willing to work for whatever commission we can agree to that is fair for both of us, and that will depend on a few things, such as...

Current market conditions, condition of the property, how much you want for the property, and how long you will give me to sell it. I'm sure when we meet you'll be amazed at how I/we do business.

D) Mr./Mrs. Seller, that's a great question. What I'm hearing you say is, you're really concerned about what you're going to net at the closing table, am I right?

E) Mr./Mrs. Seller, that will be the first thing we talk about when I see you. Our main goal is to use our proven system that will attract buyers who will pay top dollar for your home, and your main goal is to get the most money for your home, right?

F) I can definitely understand your concern. I have several commission structures. Let's find a time when we can get together and work out the numbers, so we can see what makes sense for you and your family. I'm sure, like most of my clients, you're not going to move forward unless the numbers make sense. (Close for the appointment.)

Chapter 9: Conclusion

Congratulations to you for completing this book and taking the steps necessary to make your business a success! I'm proud of you! Not everyone can work for sale by owner sellers successfully. Reading this book, you now hopefully understand that it takes more than just learning scripts and objection handlers to be successful. You must have a thick skin, some brass balls, and the courage and strength to follow through.

I want you to understand more than anything, that you CAN succeed in real estate. You can do whatever you set your mind to. Do not let anyone take that away from you. I was fortunate enough to have a father that always encouraged me and told me I could overcome anything, no matter what the obstacle. He was right.

I would like to lay down a few more tips before you go, just to drive this home, and to make you understand that no matter what prospecting method you use if you have made up your mind to succeed, **YOU WILL SUCCEED!** Remember these key ideas...

1) Believe in yourself and understand that you can do whatever you set your mind to do. Wake up early in the morning and say affirmations to yourself. Pray, meditate, or workout. Do what you need to do to obtain that peace in your mind, body, heart, and spirit before you start your day, and your whole day will be better for it.

2) Prospect, prospect, prospect! No matter if you're calling FSBO, expired listings, cold calling, or door knocking. You HAVE to put in a minimum of 10 to 20 hours of actual prospecting every week to become successful in real estate on a consistent basis. This is not busywork. This is actually talking to people on the phone or face to face and growing your business. If you're not doing this, you are not prospecting, and you are not using your time wisely.

3) Have your database get sick of you... in a good way, of course. Contact your database twice every quarter. Call them on their birthdays, anniversaries, holidays and all special events.

Once a month send them a postcard or use a service like realestatetools.com. Once a month, you could email them a neighborhood update on what homes have sold in the area, and at least once a quarter pop by their house just to say hi. Maybe even drop off a little gift if you would like.

Being successful in real estate is all about talking to people; interacting with them and helping them. Make those connections, and then grow those relationships. Put in the time and effort, and you can reap the rewards of your hard work later.

From the bottom of my heart I would like to thank each and every one of you who spent your

hard-earned money, and most of all your valuable time, supporting me and reading this book or

listening to the audible version. It shows your dedication to your craft and to your own success.

To all of you, take care, and Godspeed to everything you touch.

Thank you.

New Agents Success Guide

Become Successful with Time-Tested Proven Systems!

Special Thanks

I would like to give special thanks to 3 important individuals that helped mold my successful real estate business.

David Sheerin Broker/Owner of Century 21 Amber Realty Inc. located in Torrance California. There's a reason why the Lord puts people in your life. I always dreamed of being in real estate. Now that I'm in real estate, I have the privilege of working right next to a man that made his fortune in real estate.

Dave is definitely a man that has no problem calling it as he sees it. If you're wrong, he tells you if you're wrong, if you're right you tell you if you're right. He'll take the time out of his busy schedule to sit down with you and Mentor you with his wealth of knowledge. I credit my jump start in real estate because of him and the systems he put in place to help all of his agents to succeed. I can never thank this man enough!

David McClintock Is definitely the man I go to, to advise me about mortgages. When I first started in real estate, he held my hand walking me through the buyers' process of obtaining a mortgage, qualifying for a loan and all the pitfalls you have to avoid getting the deal closed. I'm proud to call this man my friend and my brother in real estate. Thank you for everything!!

Karl Woehrstein Co-Broker/Office Manager of Century 21 Amber Realty. When I first met Karl, he asked me, why did I want to get into real estate? I told him I wanted to make enough money to buy investment properties for retirement. He told me I could do anything I want in this world of Real Estate. And my real estate license is essentially my golden ticket or your lottery ticket. It's up to me if I was going to cash it in or not. The passion that David Sheerin And Karl have for Real Estate is reflected in their care and concern for all their agents as an agent myself I feel that.

There are so many times where I was in Karl's office where he was schooling me on real estate sales, prospecting and the sales contract. I know it's his job as a broker, but I also know it's been lots of times where he took me under his wing and truly invested his time and energy to make me a better agent because he truly cares about me as a friend. And for that, I'm truly grateful. Thank you, Karl, for putting up with me. lol

Forward

To the Realtor,

I am of the personal belief that " Home Ownership" is one of the cornerstones of Americana. Owning your own home creates Roots, Community, Stability, Equity, and security in retirement.

Helping people achieve those goals, "The American Dream", makes being a Realtor a challenging and rewarding career. A Simple task, but not always easy. This book is an ideal roadmap for your real estate career.
Good luck,

Karl Woehrstein
Realtor since 1978

Introduction

When I began my career in Real Estate, I couldn't wait to begin making my fortune. So, I started working for the number one Real Estate office in the South Bay. I still work there to this day. Before I started practicing Real Estate, I went to my Broker's training classes on Tuesdays, Thursdays, and Saturdays to learn what I needed to know before I actually dove in 110%.

I swear my broker could be a stand-up comedian if he wanted to. He was funny but serious. He would tell us, "Congratulations on passing your Real Estate exam. I want you to listen to me very carefully...vendor/vendee, lessor/lessee, grantor/grantee, I want you to understand you will never use these terms ever again in the real world of Real Estate."

When he said it, It was really funny but he also serious too. "The lifeblood of any Real Estate agent is prospecting and if you still have a full box of business cards after 3 months you have to look in the mirror and ask yourself, who are you lying to?"

The point is, my broker didn't sugar coat much. So in this book, I'm going to just go with his lead, and tell you how it really is in the game of Real Estate.

I'm going to tell you as he told me: "90% of Real Estate agents don't make any money".

When I heard that I was shocked. That's why I work harder than the average agent so I can be in the 10% that succeeds.

No matter if you're a new agent with your new shiny Real Estate license or a seasoned agent looking to restart their business when it comes down to it, you are going to have to make a decision. Are you going to do what it takes to succeed in this business?

This book is an update to my previous book *Holiday Prospecting for Dollars*. That book was designed around the holidays so you can prospect on steroids, get business, and receive those holiday closings that you and your family deserve.

However, I know there are twelve months out of the year. That's why this book was born to educate you on the techniques and strategies of prospecting all year around. With that said let me tell you a little story.

In late 2011, the economy was in the toilet and we were suffering from the worst recession since the great depression. I was in the middle of a divorce and sold my successful school bus company. I just wanted to walk away from everything and start a new life. What better way to do that than by doing something I always dreamed of...**Real Estate**.

Lo and behold, nobody told me that Real Estate is not as easy is it looks. Do not get me wrong, **Real Estate is easy, just not an easy business.**

That is exactly why I am writing this book based on the Best Seller, *Holiday Prospecting for Dollars,* this book will educate you on proven systems. If you work the system, the system will provide results.

No matter when you pick up this book, Winter, Spring, Summer, or Fall, it is a quick start, jump start, meant to get you out of a Real Estate sales slump. Let's face it, most agents are not happy with their production: getting four, ten, twenty-five, maybe a hundred deals a year. You can always do much better for you and your family. That's it...right? Family! That's why we go the extra mile. Dealing with clients who don't appreciate us, long hours at the office, babysitting Open Houses where nobody shows? There's nothing more important than family, so you know how important it is to generate business all the time.

New Agents Success Guide is designed to get you back into a Real Estate kick-ass momentum and stay there. If you are a new agent on the scene, this book is going to propel your business into the stratosphere.

I'm going to give you some keys to jump-start your mindset, your motivation, and your passion to succeed in Real Estate.

1. **Your Mindset** - We need to recalibrate your mindset as a top producer and kick out all those limiting beliefs or excuses that are clouding up what's between your ears.
2. **Hot Lead Sources** - Work on **NOW** leads sources, that will generate business now and for years to come.
3. **Taking Massive Action** - Let's take Grant Cardone's example, and 10x our actions because there's no way in hell you are going to be successful in anything you do if you do not take any action. Being a successful Real Estate Agent is all up to you. When you first start, or when you are getting over a sales slump, you are going to have to work your butt off to get back into

high gear. You need a system and a game plan that's going to feed your pipeline and grow your business to new heights.

Throughout this book, you will find little golden nuggets, proven systems, and tools that you can use for your prospecting for new business. This will help you develop your business for success. I know if you put forth the effort and the hard work that it takes to succeed, the information provided will help you in your business.

So, I would suggest, roll up your sleeves and prepare to put forth 10x action if you're serious about succeeding in Real Estate.

Let me ask you a serious question: how would you feel if you had several closings and you have some pending sales for future business right now?

How would the extra income help you and your family? I don't know about you, but I'll be excited to be kicking Real Estate ass while everyone is planning their vacation.

Let's do the right thing, pick up this book today, and let me show you how to work smarter, not harder. You can transform your Real Estate career into something you and your family will be proud of for years to come.

I'm looking forward to working with you on the other side!

Your Mindset

Okay, everyone, I want you to understand this, so I need you to get comfortable. Turn off Facebook and Twitter. Find a part in your home or office where you can relax and not be disturbed.

Now open your mind to the possibilities of increasing your business.

The first thing that we need to do is reset our thinking and our beliefs because if you don't believe in yourself, how in the hell is someone going to trust you with their most important asset? There's a reason that we're on this God-given Earth. Each one of us has our own purpose in life. Some of us know what it is, and some of us do not, but most of us will never know.

If you're reading this book, you can take control of this moment and find out what your strength is, what your weaknesses are, and turn them both around to your advantage.

As you read this book right now, I don't know what point of the year it is for you personally but I can tell you this. No matter how good or bad your year was up to this point, right now this moment you have the opportunity to change your future for the better. You have control of your future no one else.

Real Estate is the only business I know where you can make as much money as you want, and all you have to do is help as many people as you can. We get paid more than doctors, lawyers, or even brain surgeons. All we have to do for a very comfortable lifestyle is prospect three hours a day, five days a week.

Look deep down inside yourself, and ask: what motivates me?
Family, cars, money, or maybe it's just making ends meet? I can tell you from personal experience, worrying about your finances will drive you crazy, keep you up at night, and if you're not careful, kill you. That's why it's more important than ever to watch what you think and feel, or who you interact with because this will affect you in more ways than you can realize.

Energy Suckers

If you're hanging around someone that's always complaining, nagging or downright depressing, you must cut them off. They are sucking the life force out of you. I love this quote from Oprah Winfrey:

> *"You know this to be true. There are some energy suckers in your life. Just literally, taking the life force out of you. You will never be able to do or be who you supposed to be in the world as long as you continue to buy into the energy suckers."*

Guard your positive energy, your positive mindset, and your well-being as if your life depends on it because actually, it does. Your whole future in Real Estate depends on your mindset. If you claim your doubt, insecurities, and imperfections, they're going to become apparent to other people. If you claim to yourself, I am confident, I'm knowledgeable, and I'm going to do the best work possible, that also will show through to your colleagues, clients, and your family.

Keep Life Simple!

The first thing we need to do is just keep life simple. It might be easier said than done but let go and let God. Most of the things we stress over can be easily resolved if we just let it go. For example, say you're driving down the street and someone cuts you off. You're hollering and screaming at them, your blood pressure is going up, your eyes turn red, your face fills up with anger, and for what? They don't even realize what they've done, and they don't even notice that you're upset.

So, for the rest of the day, you carry this anger with you in some form or fashion. Did you know by continuously being stressed out, worried or angry, you are speeding up the aging process 2.7%? I'm sure no one wants to get old before their time.

If I need to calm down, relax, or reset my emotional clock, I have this relaxation technique I use. The cool thing about this technique is it works well for people that suffer from panic attacks, anxiety, or in any situation where you need to calm down.

When you feel yourself getting angry or super anxious, this is the best time to start this technique.

1. Take a deep breath through your mouth and fill your lungs up with air, as much as possible, and hold it.

2. At the same time, you're holding your breath, you need to tense up all your muscles all over your body from your toes, legs, midsection, neck, and face. Tense everything for five to ten seconds and hold.

3. After the five to ten seconds are up, relax and let the air out of your body steadily.

I know you're probably saying to yourself, "This Real Estate guy is crazy."

I thought so too when it was first introduced to me, but after I did it, I was amazed by the wave of tension, stress, and fear that just left my body immediately.

Like anything it takes practice, and when I first started doing it, sometimes I would have to do it two or three times to get the full effect. As time went on, certain things did not trigger my anger or my anxiety anymore.

Just changing your mindset and your thinking toward certain things and getting in the habit of letting things go will take time, even with the help of this technique, but trust me, you will feel better in the long term.

Do you have a Morning Routine?

What type of morning routine do you have? Did you know most people wake up just early enough to get ready and go to work? That's barely enough time to wash up, brush your teeth, have a decent bathroom run, change into your clothes, and run out the door. This throws off your day because you're always playing catch up.

I've been in transportation for over twenty years and I know the highest probable time to have a car accident is before 9 a.m. and after 5 p.m., Monday through Friday, excluding holidays.

That's a different beast altogether. Most of the accidents in the morning are because people are running late, and they are trying to shave off time. They're cutting you off, running lights, and driving recklessly. I'm sure you noticed it.

Do this: change your morning routine.

Why don't you wake up an hour, NO, two hours early, every morning? It's like you have a head start on the world. Yeah, it's going to take some getting used to, but you'll notice right off the bat how things look new and different when you wake up a little early. You don't feel so rushed, you can relax, pray, meditate, or read a good book. When you're driving to the office, you notice the lighter traffic. People are not in such a rush, and it sets the pace for your day. I like that saying, it's never crowded when you go the extra mile. So, let's do this, Wake up a few minutes earlier every day, and let me know how it works for you. Ok?

Exercise

Okay, let's talk about exercise! Exercise is the number one way to make you feel better. Yes, I know, sometimes it's hard. You feel sad, depressed lethargic, lazy, and the list goes on and on. Let's face it, you don't have to be a scientist to know exercise is good for you. It keeps your weight in check and makes you physically fit and stronger. Working out keeps you feeling youthful and active and keeps obesity and its diseases at bay. With continuous exercise, you can most likely live a nice active life into old age.

Another advantage I love about exercise is it helps you with your mindset by improving the way you feel. Exercise actually makes you a happier person and relieves your stress. I don't know the technical jargon. Let's just say it releases happy chemicals into your brain.

This helps you with anxiety and stress. My personal example comes from when I was going through a tough time during my divorce. I noticed myself working out more. I found myself less stressed after a workout. I was able to think clearly and make better decisions.

When you exercise, it stresses your body at a low level by raising your breathing, heart rate, and exhausting your muscles to a certain extent. Of course, it depends on which exercises you do and how long the session lasts. With continuous exercise, you will eventually condition your whole body and mind to better handle life's stresses. Less stress equals a better quality of life!

I'm just going to put it out there: I'm insecure about how I look, and I know I'm not the only one. When you exercise and eat right, that weight starts slowly burning off. Yes, it's hard work, but when you start seeing the scale reading lower numbers, that boosts your self-confidence, makes you feel better, and makes you want to work harder to reach your goals.

If you purchased this book, most likely we're in the same industry: Real Estate! You can relate to my crazy mixed-up world that's never the same from one day to the next. I'm going to give you three tips to make it easier for you to put that Sweat Equity in getting your body, mind, and soul in shape:

1. **Schedule your workouts** - As a successful Real Estate Agent, you should be scheduling everything: prospecting, appointments, and workouts should be no different. Once you actively put it in your schedule, you won't be able to miss it. It's locked in. Set the dates, time, duration, and what type of workout it will be, so when it pops up on your calendar, you're prepared.

   I know different agents work out at different times during the day. I personally love working out in the morning before the sun comes up. There is just something about a brand-new morning and having that brand-new feeling of life.

2. **Workout posse or friends** - It's always better to work out with friends, so talk to other Agents in your office, friends, or relatives. Work on that support network, so that way you'll have a higher level of staying power through accountability. When you're working out with friends or a group, there is just something about the energy of others that helps your self-esteem to build you up and increase your motivation.

3. **Just do it** - I love those Nike commercials. Just do it! Find your greatness. If you don't know what I'm talking about, just go on YouTube and do a search. You will be inspired. To move ahead in this world, you must take action, so no more excuses or putting it off.

The best way to be prepared for your exercise is to have your clothes ready the night before. Whenever you work out, have a workout bag with a change of clothes. That way when you're ready to hit the gym, you're all set.

Having a good playlist to listen to can be a motivator as well. If you would like to see what I use or where I work out, just check out my YouTube channel: https://www.youtube.com/channel/UCXxXrnEm4jxa_TtDs73Xjuw (Search "willie j may enterprises" on YouTube).

Hopefully, this will motivate you to act, and once you do, you will feel much better about yourself, your health, and your future.

Hot Lead Sources

There are countless lead sources out there for a Real Estate Agent to choose from. There's no time to be distracted. We need to hyper-focus our lead generation efforts to generate business now and narrow our focus on certain lead sources that will generate a high probability of success.

It's like we're a sniper zeroing in on our target, unlike most agents who are using the shotgun technique praying they will hit something. We have a goal in mind: target immediate and continuous business.

We're going to focus our prospecting efforts on:

- Expired Listings
- For Sale By Owners
- FSBO Open Houses
- Past clients
- SOI/Databases

For this system, we are mainly looking for listings rather than working with buyers. If you run across a buyer that is motivated, meaning a buyer who is going to follow your instructions and has a definite time frame on purchasing a home, then definitely work with that buyer. If not, refer that buyer out for a referral fee.

Expired Listings

The always popular Expired Listings. Expired Listings are the number one source of immediate business for any Real Estate Agent. They've been on the market for over six months and haven't sold. There could be several reasons why the home didn't sell: bad location, substandard condition, falling apart, no showings, no lockbox for easy accessibility, and the number one reason, the property is overpriced.

One of the good things about Expired Listings is that a highly successful Real Estate Agent will lay the foundation and inform the sellers about what is needed to sell a house in their market. In most cases, those listings will not expire.

What works in our favor is most Expired Listings are expired because the Agent wasn't strong enough to inform their client about what needs to be done to get their property sold for top dollar. As a result, the property expires, and the clients are upset because they wasted six months of their lives just to be that much farther away from their goals and dreams of moving on with their lives.

Our job is getting in front of the Expired Listing and letting them know that we're the authority on getting their home sold for top dollar. If they are still motivated to move, then we should do whatever we can to stay in front of them. When the time is right, we get hired and do what is necessary to get their property sold and have happy clients.

For Sale by Owners

These are the DIY people who love doing everything on their own. After it doesn't work, they call a professional to clean it up. FSBOs are just regular people like you and me that are either trying to do it on their own just to see if they can, or they are trying to save some cash just as you or I would on an expensive purchase.

When you go to a car lot, you know you are going to have to haggle, so you try to do your homework because you know it's going to be a fight when you talk to the salesman. If you aren't careful, you will be driving off into the sunset with buyer's remorse.

As Real Estate Agents, we already don't have the most pristine reputation. Be mindful when you interact with potential clients. Always be professional, courteous, and let them know without a shadow of a doubt that you know exactly how to get their home sold.

FSBO Open Houses

Say what? For Sale By Owner Open Houses! I understand a lot of Agents haven't heard of this practice or are unwilling to utilize this technique, but our main purpose is to jump-start our business. What better way to jump-start our business than work with FSBO's looking to sell now.

By providing the FSBO with helpful information on how to sell the property by themselves, after a while they'll realize it's not as easy as it seems to sell a house. By offering them help on an extra level with Open Houses, you put yourself in the position where you can possibly double the transaction, or at the bare minimum, get some good leads on some buyers looking to buy right now. So, For Sale By Owner Open Houses work very well as a shot of adrenaline to your Real Estate business.

Sphere of Influence (SOI)/Database

Your sphere of influence or your database consists of:

- Friends
- Family
- Acquaintances
- Past clients
- Current clients
- Neighbors

The list goes on and on. The short definition is, **Everyone You Know.** Let's think about this for a minute. It's not only everyone you know, but it's also everyone you know that knows you sell Real Estate.

Ask yourself: of all the people you know, how many of them know you sell Real Estate?

If you're thinking to yourself, "Hmmm...not so many", then it looks like we have some work to do.

Taking Massive Action

"The graveyard is the richest place on earth, because it is here that you will find all the hopes and dreams that were never fulfilled, the books that were never written, the songs that were never sung, the inventions that were never shared, the cures that were never discovered, all because someone was too afraid to take that first step, keep with the problem, or determined to carry out their dream."
– Les Brown

How bad do you want to be successful? Are you willing to put in the effort for what it takes to be a successful Realtor? If you really consider the lives of successful individuals throughout history, you'll see they invested a massive amount of time building their business. We all know success does not come overnight. One of the best advantages that we have in the Real Estate industry is that success can be duplicated.

Let me say this again just in case you didn't catch it the first time: **success can be duplicated**.

If you have the directions to the destination, you will succeed. Now following those directions may be a problem. Life might get in the way, self-doubt, lack of motivation, any number of things might get in the way. That's why I asked you how bad you want to be successful. The thing is if you want it bad enough, you'll make it happen. I believe in you and I know you can be successful. All you have to do is invest in yourself with some old-fashioned hard work.

Focus on the Basics

Avoidance behavior, scared to get started, self-doubt, not knowing what to say, not having the courage to push through...understand that we all go through these emotions when we are new. Sometimes when we are seasoned veterans, these insecurities may creep back in because we're complacent about our business.

We don't have to have the greatest mind on the planet to succeed in Real Estate. Just be consistent! By turning your attention to, and focusing on the basics, you will be able to build a successful foundation in Real Estate.

Let me tell you how...

One of the main characteristics of a successful agent is communication, right? You and I can agree most of us are not born as exceptional communicators. What this means is that good communication or having any good dialogue with your client must be learned, practiced, and rehearsed, so you can get good, great, and eventually reach the point of mastery.

For you to close more deals, you have to be prepared for the opportunities. At the beginning of my career, I lost many transactions because I did not know the proper words to say. I just did not have the experience that was needed to lock down the listing.

It happened to me; it will happen to you. It's just part of the learning process. I guess you could say it's like on-the-job training because every situation and transaction are different. If a situation or transaction knocks you flat on your back, learn from that, get up, dust yourself off, and move on to the next deal. Your mistakes, your situations, your customers, and all the learning experience that you face in business and in life will make you a better Real Estate Agent for yourself and for your customers. When you make a mistake, do not beat yourself up. Learn from it and move on. You'll be a better agent as a result.

I would suggest working on your scripts in the morning just before you hit the phones and before any other prospecting activity. If you're new in the business, I would suggest practicing/role-playing for forty-five minutes to an hour every day before each session.

If you've been a Real Estate Agent for a while and you're familiar with your scripts, I still suggest you practice for at least fifteen to thirty minutes before each prospecting session. I don't know how many times I knew what to say, but for some reason, my mind went blank for that split-second and the client hung up on me. Consistently practicing your scripts is mastering the basics.

The more you practice the better you become. Practicing with different role play partners will build up your confidence and your stamina for prospecting.

If you're scared of calling or you have call reluctance, try out this schedule for a twelve-hour call session:

Call from 8:00 a.m. until 8:00 p.m. Have two breaks of ten minutes each in the morning. Take an hour for lunch. Take two more ten-minute breaks before 5 p.m. Take a forty-five-minute break, and finish out your session at 8:00 p.m.

I will guarantee you that you'll be completely physically and mentally exhausted from cold calling, but this is like getting tried by fire. This is well worth the education that you will learn by doing a marathon session.

In this twelve-hour session, you probably made more contacts and dials then most agents do in their first years in the business. On top of that great feat, you now have more confidence and determination to be successful. Now with this newly developed confidence, you can talk to anybody. You will soon see your business go to the next level.

GOLDEN NUGGET: Always use your sales stats. If not yours, then the stats of your company. You can also use the surrounding neighborhood sales stats as well. Remind them of their motivation to sell, and that you have a proven system to get the job done.

The Game Plan Part 1

The real estate business is not a quick race. It is a marathon. You have to set up your business like a business. When someone goes to a traditional job, they go 9 to 5. When successful entrepreneurs start their business, they put their blood, sweat, and tears into it to be successful. Read any successful person's biography: Thomas Edison, Steve Jobs, Bill Gates. All of these men and so many others put in hard work and dedication to be successful.

You're no longer an employee. As a real estate agent, you are an independent contractor. In other words, you're an entrepreneur. It's up to you how successful you want to be in this business. You just have to decide how much you are willing to sacrifice to succeed. I have said this so many times in this book and my other books: **"Real Estate is easy, but not an easy business."**

In my opinion, the key to becoming a successful real estate agent is all about having the determination to prospect continuously for new business. **Prospecting is the lifeblood of any real estate agent.** There are two types of prospecting:

1. **Sweat Equity**: This form of prospecting takes little or no cash. It's all about cold calling, door knocking, and Open Houses just to name a few. It has been proven that prospecting continuously over time will generate you a very nice income no matter where in the United States you are located. **The secret is being consistent.**

2. **Prospecting with Cold Hard Cash:** Of course, prospecting with the mighty dollar will generate business, but it is very expensive. This form of prospecting could look like buying advertisements on Zillow, Realtor.com, Trulia, and Redfin just to name a few. One thing I must remind you that most agents do not realize, if you're buying leads, no matter what they tell you **those leads are not exclusively yours.** Those clients are searching for multiple websites and filling out multiple forms. By understanding this, you will understand that when you follow up with those leads, you will seldom be the only agent that's contacting them.

I know many fellow agents who prefer prospecting with cash as opposed to prospecting with sweat equity because it's easy to pull out the plastic and just charge it. Remember my broker Karl and what he said to me in class?

"90% of Real Estate agents don't make any money".

They assume when they get into the business it will be easy. On top of that, you have all these lead vultures and real estate gurus calling you trying to sell you a magic bullet or some leads. There you go, pulling out the plastic and charging it. Before most real estate agents make their first sale, they're being sold on some kind of gimmick.

I take this personally because it has happened to me. If it wasn't for my broker, Karl, I would have lost even more money. Please believe me when I tell you. **"It doesn't take much money to be successful in real estate, just hard work, and determination."**

The Game Plan Part 2

I truly believe in the real estate business. An agent has to evolve in order to make it in this business. There are different stages of real estate agents. I like to call it, The Evolution of a Successful Real Estate Agent. There's the New Agent, the Seasoned Agent, the Investor Agent, and the Passive Income Agent. I'll talk more about these stages of agents in the chapter **Do you have a real estate business Exit Strategy?**

In this book and all my books, I make it a point to double down on having a strategy or a proven system. You can even call it a Game Plan for how to run your business and generate and nurture your leads. In this particular book, *New Agent Success Guide*, I go over several different ways to generate and follow up on your leads. I'm about to go over two basic systems that if done consistently will grow your business. It does not matter if you are a new agent, a seasoned agent, or an agent just trying to restart their career. Let's dig in!

The first strategy we're going to go over is a basic follow-up strategy. This strategy is so simple and boring that it's difficult for most agents. I adopted this strategy from a very successful broker in Southern California named Neil Schwartz. I've learned a great deal from Neil from his free YouTube channel. Check him out!

I have one of his quote framed on my wall: **"90% of what's wrong in your life today.....can be cured by MASSIVE prospecting."** - Neil Schwartz

In mid-2015, Neil did a webinar that changed my outlook on prospecting and follow-up forever. As an active agent, I put my own little spin on it and added: "pop by once every 6 months". Studies have shown if you meet with people face-to-face you build a better connection and relationship. Not to mention, I was taught by my broker, Karl, to get out of the office and meet people. **Belly to Belly Face to Face,** Is the number one way to get people to know you, like you, and trust you.

The Super Simple Follow-up System:

For this system, we're using easy numbers. For example, we're starting off with 100 contacts. My definition of contact for the system is...

- Full Name
- Home or property address

- Home phone or cell phone or both
- Email address
- Social media, Examples: LinkedIn, Facebook, Twitter.
- Special dates: Home purchase anniversary, wedding anniversary, Family member birthdays, pet birthdays. You'll be surprised how many families celebrate Little Skipper's birthday.

You may be a new agent, so work with what you have. As time goes on and you interact with your clients or potential clients, you can add the necessary information into your database with regular conversation. Eat the elephant one little piece at a time.

If you are an existing agent, you're already ahead of the curve. The most common problem with existing agents is cleaning up their database. I would suggest that you just start with your top 100 contacts and go from there with the system. The super-simple follow-up system is very simple to implement and master. It is designed to start anywhere throughout the year and it's just about I would say dummy-proof. As most of my friends can tell you, I'm a big dummy.

The Game Plan Part 3

The secret sauce we're working with is 100 contacts to start.

- Email weekly something free, timely and pertinent
- Snail mail monthly
- Give them a call every 90 days
- Pop by their home or property once every 6 months

Like I mentioned before, this is a super simple follow-up system. In the upcoming chapters, I will show you what tools and techniques I use for staying in contact with my contacts in my database. You'd be surprised to know most of the top real estate agents who stay in contact with their sphere of influence and database use a system similar to this one we're about to dive into.

Time to get down and dirty. Draw a line on a piece of blank paper oriented in landscape to represent your current year up to 10 years in the future. In this example, I started with 2021. If you're working the system and assuming that you will stay in contact with 100 contacts per year, it's safe to say that you can close 10% of that business, give or take.

Using this system, you should be able to directly or indirectly close 10 deals from your database. If you contact 200 contacts, that should go up approximately to 20 closed transactions per year and so on.

Every real estate market is different but, in this example, we're going with $10,000 per closed transaction just to make the numbers simple. I like simple!

Whatever time you decide to do your prospecting, make sure you allocate enough time to contact enough people in your database to stay on target. Later on, in this book. I will share with you the contact management software and the systems and strategies I use that helped me in my prospecting.

Here's the simple math for year one in our example, 2021. By contacting 100 contacts and closing 10% or 10 transactions at $10,000 each, one would earn $100,000 in commission.

I hope you see how I got this. Let me explain. If the average commission in your area is $10,000 gross per transaction and you close 10 deals. That equals $100,000.

By contacting 200 contacts and closing 20 at $10,000 each, one would earn $200,000 that year.

We added 100 more contacts to our database to reach the 100 contacts per year goal. We need to add 8 contacts per month. That equals 96 contacts per year. But we're rounding it up to 100 contacts. Is it starting to make sense? Of course! I told you it was super simple.

By 2023, we are contacting 300 contacts and closing 30 at $10,000 each to earn $300,000 for the year.

I hope you're starting to get excited. We're not doing anything crazy like spending money on ads or anything like that in this example. Basically, all you're doing is prospecting like you normally would for business calling expireds, For Sale By Owners, conducting Open Houses, and adopting good forsaken leads that need an agent. Each month, all you have to add at minimum is 8 contacts per month. You can find at least 8 good contacts a month, can't you? I know you can!

Year	Contacts	Deals Closed	Commission
2021	100	10	$100,000
2022	200	20	$200,000
2023	300	30	$300,000
2024	400	40	$400,000
2025	500	50	$500,000
2026	600	60	$600,000
2027	700	70	$700,000
2028	800	80	$800,000
2029	900	90	$900,000
2030	1000	100	$1,000,000

As you can see in 2030, we moved up to 1,000 contacts, 100 deals closed, and that generates $1,000,000 for that year. Congratulations!!! If you followed the system and you stuck with it, you're now a million-dollar producing agent! All you had to do was prospect for new business like you should and add at least 8 contacts to your database per month. Just work the system as stated before, which was:

- Email weekly something free, timely and pertinent
- Snail mail monthly
- Give them a call every 90 days

- Pop-By to their home or property once every 6 months

This Super Simple Follow-up System! It's not sexy. It does not have any fancy frills, fancy lights, or cool gimmicks. It's basically a down-to-earth system that works if you work the system. As you read on, in this book, I give you tools and resources with techniques so when you're making your calls and interacting with your clients, everything will fall into place. I'm reiterate I'm not guaranteeing you any specific results. I'm just sharing with you a proven system that has worked for me and many other agents. With that said, let's move on to prospecting with cash!

The Game Plan Part 4

Prospecting with Cold Hard Cash! There are several different ways to invest your money into your business. One of the most popular ways is what I call **Buying Leads:** Zillow, Realtor.com, Trulia and so on. In this section, we're not going to go down that slippery slope. I'm going to share with you a basic system that I've seen many top agents use. From what I can see, most of the time prospecting with cash is the only prospecting that they do. Surprisingly this technique seems to work well for them.

In most cases, these agents have a geographical farm or ranch. Let me back up for a minute. A geographical farm is a neighborhood or subdivision with a few homes or a few hundred homes. A geographical ranch is a neighborhood or community with over a thousand homes.

I made a good portion of my business through farming, but when I farm, I use a different tactic. I door-knock my farm and I get to know the community. My farm was close to 800 homes including three subdivisions. If I stick to my schedule, I can door-knock my whole farm inside of three months. When I door-knock, I give them a newsletter with a notepad. That's my basic system. There are other things I do to prospect my farm, but this system was basically low cost, high sweat equity, and high returns!

The top-producing agents that I know who are successful with spending cash for prospecting have a certain neighborhood they market to. They can market to a few hundred homes or a few thousand homes. It all depends on their budget.

They usually send some sort of market update attached to market evaluation. The market evaluation is usually a website with a capture page. This is so they can collect the potential client's information when they're requesting their home evaluation.

The information they send to their farm could vary from a small postcard to an 8 1/2 by 11 mailer.

I found out very quickly when I spoke to these agents that they safeguarded their secrets very carefully. When I inquired about their advertisements, the companies they used, and the frequency they mailed, it was like pulling teeth. They just did not want to give up the goose that laid the golden eggs.

In the research of my market, the top-producing agents that just mailed their farm areas and did no other prospecting, made between $100,000 to $300,000 a year. That's a decent amount of change in my book. Just a reminder, I'm located in the highly expensive Southern California Market.

I was curious to know how much they were spending on advertising. One agent did tell me that he uses EDDM. That stands for Every Door Direct Mail. It's a service is from the United States Postal Service (USPS). He informed me that he sends something out of value every two weeks and he's been doing this for over 10 years. It's been way more cost-effective in the last few years since Every Door Direct Mail has taken effect but a lot more work setting up the mailers. There are other online direct mail services out there. Take the time and investigate prices and services that best suit your budget and your business model.

One of the things you need to understand is, when you're advertising to a farm area, you're spending money. You must look at it like you're investing in yourself and the community. Don't expect your phone to be ringing off the hook when you send out your first round of mailers. Be prepared to invest a good amount of time and a few months of advertising on your farm before you see results.

You will have a quicker response time if you do additional prospecting in your farm area such as cold calling and door knocking. This helps put a face to the name. To get more bang for your buck if you don't have any listings on your farm, I would suggest that you call other agents to see if you can do an open house and get permission to advertise the open house. This will help immensely in having you recognized as the neighborhood expert.

Even though I couldn't get other agents to share how much they were spending on advertising, they did share with me their mailing schedule for their advertisements. They all basically had the same technique. This is my take on the information I received for the best possible results when you are prospecting with cash in your farm:

1. Don't bite off more than you can chew. Start off small.

2. Start off with 50 to 100 homes if that's comfortable for you and grow from there.

3. Choose your mailing frequency. In the beginning, I would suggest mailing out to your farm once every quarter. When you start closing deals, move up to monthly. Once you feel your business is to the point where it makes financial sense, you can start growing your farm by 50-75 home increments. Once you feel your farm is a decent size, then increase your mailing frequency to every two weeks.

4. Remember to keep it super simple. I would suggest using a company that specializes in mailing into neighborhoods. I recommend corefact.com.

5. Make a commitment to farming success. Research and see how much you need to advertise for one whole year. Before you start the process, make sure that you have what you need in the bank or pay the year of advertising in advance. By doing this step, you highly advance your percentages of success.

6. Understand this process takes time. So do not rush it. Do whatever you can to help the process along by doing other prospecting.

This is just to give you another option for prospecting. I just want to warn you. When you pay for shortcuts and they don't work out, that puts you and your business on Dangerous Ground. Be careful and understand your business depends on your wise choices. Now let's get into expired listings!

Expired Listings

Nothing gets me more excited than receiving highly motivated leads each morning when I log into my computer. First off, I'm if you have a contact management system, that you're using to retrieve your leads and store them. If you would like recommendations, you can check out my book *Top 10 Expired Objections* - http://amzn.to/2zdYnYY.

I understand that if you've been in the business for a while you're set on your own style of prospecting. However, if you're new in the business, you probably do not have a clue where to begin. No problem, I have your back.

What we're going to do is set a small goal. In this way, you can achieve that goal and be successful. No matter when you start your commitment to prospecting, you must have a made-up mind and a commitment to 10X your prospecting for thirty days. Thirty days is not that long and not that short.

Look at it like this: the small steps you make every day transform into the compound effect. It will build up over time. Each day you do money-making activities is a higher chance that you get rewarded in the future. Each day counts and each contact counts. Do not take your relationship for granted. That is future potential income.

Working with Expired Listings, you must make sure that you have a game plan including a contact method with which you're comfortable. My contact method of choice is the telephone, but there are other contact methods as well. This is my list in order of effectiveness:

- Door knocking
- Phone calls
- Direct Mail

Expired Door Knocking

Door knocking is one of the most effective ways to go after an Expired Listing. The reason is that there are not that many highly motivated Real Estate Agents going after Expired Listings on a 10x scale, much less picking up the phone and calling.

I said it before, and I'll say it again: **belly to belly, face to face**.

It's the number one best method of prospecting.

When you talk to the Expired Listing, most likely they're going to be impressed that you are taking the extra steps to offer your services to help them and their family move forward.

When you go to the Expired door, make sure you're prepared with a pre-list package or some sort of tri-fold brochure that has your information on it, how you do business, and your testimonials to give to the potential client. This next part is very important: make sure that the information you're giving them is on high-quality paper because remember, you're a higher-class Agent! You must demonstrate it accordingly.

If you're new to the business and you do not have promotional material for yourself, I would suggest that you have your brokerage, or a fellow agent help you. If you do not have past clients, fall back on the satisfied clients of your brokerage. Ask your broker if it's okay to use some of the company's satisfied clients as testimonials.

When you go door-to-door for Expired Listings, one the many things you want to look for is if there are absentee owners or is the property owner-occupied? You need to know which one is which. You don't want to be pulling up to an Expired Listing and knocking on the door to a renter at seven or eight in the morning. That's not going to be a very good experience at all.

Make sure you do your homework. An absentee owner is a homeowner that owns the property but lives in a different location. Owner-occupied property is when the homeowner actually lives in the home. Our strategy is to go after both, but we do it the correct way. When you identify the absentee owner, make a note of the property that has Expired and the current resident. With an owner-occupied property, you know you can contact the seller directly by going straight to the property.

Another thing I would suggest when you're knocking on those Expired doors is to always be prepared. Always have a few blank copies of the listing agreement with you. You won't get the listing every time, but you always want to be prepared. If the opportunity presents itself, take the listing right then and there. It will happen. You must be prepared for it.

Expired Door Knocking Script:

Script for when you're at the Expired Listing door:

My name is William with Super Agent Realty. Good morning Mr. Seller.

Seller: Good morning.

My report shows your home was for sale, but somehow left the market unsold. Is this correct?

Seller: Yes.

I'm sorry to hear that. There have been six homes in the area that sold while your home was on the market, so we know that homes are selling. If you were able to get your price and be under contract in the next two to three weeks, would that be of interest to you?

Seller: Yes.

Great I can definitely sell your house. Let's do this I'm going to go to the office, do my homework on your property, and come back today at 3 p.m. Will you be home?

This is not being pushy this is being in authority, and sure of yourself. This demonstrates your professionalism. You're demonstrating that you can sell their house. People respect that.

Seller: Yes.

If the seller says no but has another time, make yourself available for that time to take the listing.

Great, what's your best email address?

This way I can send you some information about me, my company, and how I sell homes differently than other Agents. I'll also bring my real and accurate past client testimonials.

If this is a brand-new Expired, let them know they're going to be bombarded with phone calls from other Agents looking to take the listing. Always remember your main goal when contacting Expireds is setting the appointment. Once you have the appointment set for your return and the email address, then ask the pre-qualification questions if the conversation permits:

- Where are you moving to?
- How soon do you want to have this home sold?
- Realistically, how much would you like to sell the house for?
- What do you think caused your home not to sell?

You can probably ask a million more pre-qualification questions, but we want to keep the interaction short, brief, and to the point when we are door knocking.

Understand that door knocking is very effective, but also very time-consuming. After you make contact, decide on the status of the contact. What I mean is discerning if the contact is worth following up or if it's just trash. The quicker you can categorize the prospect, the quicker you can move on to the next property.

DOOR KNOCKING BONUS TIP: If you want to 10x your door-knocking efforts and obtain a few more listings, prospect old Expireds; Expireds going back six, eight, or twenty-four months back. When you siphon through them, separate the good from the bad, the sold from the unsold, and ones with numbers from ones without.

For the ones without numbers that are not listed, those are the perfect prospects to go to the door and show them your USP or Unique Selling Proposition that should be included in your well-built, pre-list package.

Most of the time, the Expired Listing is not current on the recent Market activity. When they expired, they were overpriced or there was some other reason that caused them to expire. If it's been a few months or even a few years since they've been on the market, their home has most likely gained equity and the value has increased. You can show them that being sold at that price is more of a reality now.

Calling the Expired Listings

To catch the new Expired, you must be one of the first agents to contact them in the morning. Make it a ritual to be in your office or your home office ready to make calls no later than 7:45 a.m. I learned a long time ago that when you're the first person to give them a call, you have an 80% better chance of setting the appointment if they are still motivated to sell. If you're not one of the first ones to contact the Expireds, your percentage goes way down.

In my experience, contacting Expireds and having an actual, beneficial, positive, friendly, conversation most often occurs between 7:45 and 8:30 a.m. After that, all hell breaks loose. Why? Because while you're having a conversation with the Expired Listing, you notice other people are calling while you're trying to have that conversation. You definitely know who's calling at 8:00 a.m., right? Yes! It's your competition!

Usually, by 8:30 or 9:00 AM, they are fed up. Their phones have been ringing off the hook constantly. At this point, they either take the phone off the hook, turn off their ringer, or just simply don't answer. If they do answer, prepare to be cussed out and called all sorts of names that are not on your birth certificate. We, as Agents, understand why they're upset. They had their house on the market, and for whatever reason, it did not sell.

Suddenly, out of the blue, we're calling them trying to take the listing. In their minds, it does not make any sense. They are thinking, "Where were all these agents when I had my house on the market before?"

To understand the seriousness of this, let me tell you this story:

I was already in my second hour of prospecting on a Saturday morning. It was the first day of the month and everyone knows or should know, if the first day of the month falls on a weekend, that's the very best day to prospect Expired Listings. You have less competition because it's the weekend, and you have a higher contact rate. More people are off during the weekend, so it's a win-win. You still have competition but not as much.

Back to the story: I was making my calls and it sounded like an older lady answering the phone. It also sounded like her voice was cracking. What became apparent moments into my script was that she was trying to communicate, but her crying was getting in the way of her trying to speak to me.

The woman was crying and highly stressed. She could barely communicate at all during the first few minutes or so of the call. After I realized she was crying, I tried my best to console her by asking what was wrong and if there was anything I could do.

After she was able to calm down a little bit, she said, "I wish you damn Agents would stop calling me and leave me the hell alone. The house is not for sale, so don't call me anymore."

Right after she made her statement, she promptly hung up on me. I did not hesitate and dialed her right back. Surprisingly she answered, and before she could cuss me out or fuss at me, I said, "Ma'am, ma'am, I know you're going through a tough time right now, I just want to know what's going on to see how I can help."

She replied with a stoner tone and said, "Can you bring my husband back from the dead?"

That took me by surprise. I was silent.
"Of course not," she said.

After I gained my composure, I said, "I need to take a break from work right now, and it seems like you need someone to talk to. I have thirty minutes or so if you would like to talk and tell me what's going on. Maybe afterward, we can see if I can help you or not. If not, at least you have someone to talk to for a few minutes, and you're able to avoid all those callers harassing you. What do you say...I'm all yours."

She began to talk and told me how her husband died of a stroke a few months earlier and how hard it had been on her and her family. They were married for over forty years, and now with him gone, it was just her and the mortgage.

The only way to preserve the equity they built together in the house was to sell it. For forty years, her husband handled all the finances. Since he's been gone, she has fallen behind on the mortgage. Since the property didn't sell, she is in danger of foreclosure. She had no one to help or guide her, and the previous Agent just slapped the property on the market with an overpriced price tag. Of course, it expired.

After talking with her about an hour and a half, she became more relaxed and open-minded. I was completely honest, and I told her I understood what she was going through. I told her that I wasn't sure I could help, but the first thing I could do was come look at her house and tell her exactly why it hadn't sold. I planned to share my proven plan to get her home listed and sold. I let her know that it wouldn't cost her anything, it would only take a few minutes, and that this wasn't my first rodeo.

I met her at the house later that day and I told her that in the condition it was in, it was not surprising her home did not sell. However, I was pretty sure with a few changes, we could sell the house faster and for more money than before.

Long story short, I had someone come cut her grass and clean up the backyard. We painted the outside of the house as well as the inside. After everything was complete, I relisted the property with a detailed description and at least forty professional pictures. Within twenty-four hours we received multiple offers and the property sold $6,000 over list price. I also added another raving fan to my database.

I'm telling you this story because it doesn't matter if you're new in the business, or if you have little to no experience. You have your brokerage and your fellow Agents that support you. Maybe you have been in the business for a while, and you're nervous about calling Expireds. You need to understand we're here to help people. In the story, I took the extra steps to help somebody in need. Don't chase after the mighty dollar.

> *"You will get all you want in life if you help enough other people get what they want."* –Zig Ziglar

You probably hear this all the time, and I know I've said it a few times: prospecting is a numbers game. You must call quite a few Expireds to get through to the golden nuggets. That's why they call it prospecting.

Expired Calling Script:

> My name is William with Super Agent Realty. Good morning Mr. Seller.

> **Seller:** Good morning.

> My report shows your home was for sale, but somehow left the market unsold. Is this correct?

> **Seller:** Yes.

> For the right price, are you still interested in selling?

> **Seller:** Yes.

I specialize in helping homeowners that were on the market but didn't sell for whatever reason. I would love to see how I can help. I'm available today at 5 or would 6:30 be better for your schedule?

Seller: 6 p.m.

Sounds great, what is your best email address? I would like to send you information about me, my company, and how I do business differently than other Agents. Also, you can read the testimonials of my past clients.

After you get the email, move forward to the pre-qualification questions.

Keep the conversation short, sweet, and to the point. At the same time, try to build rapport by letting them talk 80% of the time while you talk 20% of the time with questions.

Direct Mail Campaigns

The advantage of direct mail is that you can contact the homeowner if they don't live in the area or reside out-of-state. Send them a letter letting them know that you're the neighborhood expert, and then send out a newsletter once a month with updates on current sales in their area.

You can mail different materials from newsletters to postcards to magazines. It's amazing how creative you can be with direct mail. Be careful because postage can get expensive.

Like any other form of prospecting, direct mail is a numbers game. If you run a direct mail campaign during an election and/or the holidays, understand you *will* run the risk of getting your direct mail campaigns lost in the shuffle.

In my experience, Agents who don't prospect door-to-door or via telephone usually lean on direct mail. Several times, I've arrived at an appointment with an Expired Listing to find a mountain of mail from other Agents all over the counter soliciting for their business.

My advice is if you decide to use direct mail as a part of your Expired prospecting, that you do so in conjunction with door knocking and cold calling. You can't build a rapport with a potential client through the mail. You must establish a connection.

Take the time to write a thank-you note after you speak with them. Many times, I receive a call saying thanks for the card, and that makes me feel good. I want to work that much harder.

It's not often we get thank you cards anymore. Everything is email or instant messenger. Sometimes snail mail still brings a smile to someone's face. In most cases, my experience is that it solidifies the business relationship.

I also use Send Out Cards. I love Send Out Cards because you can customize the card whatever way you like. I will take a picture of the property and have a sold banner across it. I send it to the client and let them know this can be them in the future.

Expired Follow-Up:

Did you know 80% of Real Estate Agents do not follow up on their leads? If you are spending all your time hunting down the prospect, having a good conversation with them, building rapport, and you don't follow up, you're wasting your damn time. You've probably heard this before, but I will say it again, so you can get it ingrained in your brain because you *must* understand this to be successful: **The money is in the follow-up!**

Yes, we're on the subject of expired follow-up, but follow-up needs to be done in all forms of prospecting including cold calling, Expireds, For Sale By Owners, SOI, & your beloved database.

You must exercise frequent, consistent, continuous, persistent follow-up. Each time you follow up, you build layers upon layers of rapport, and with that, TRUST. Depending on your market, it takes anywhere from eight to fifteen contacts for you to set an appointment just so you have the opportunity to present. Do you know your competition will contact Expireds one or two times, maybe even three times on a good day?

The good thing about being in Quarter Four is that most of your competition will be taking off on vacation, slacking off, or just quit the business until the first of the year. As I mentioned earlier in the book, every day you have new listings in your market. When you have less competition that increases your likelihood to acquire more listings. If you don't put in the work necessary to follow up on these Expired gems, the top-producing agents in your market know the value of follow-up. When you don't follow up, it's like giving your money away to them. So, do the follow-up work that needs to be done, and get yourself on their radar.

The Expired Follow-Up System

My expired follow-up system is simple. The first thing I do is kick call reluctance to the curb because there's no space for me not to make my calls. I need to support my family and I'm working very hard to achieve my financial dreams. Knowing that each time I have a closing in my market, I receive a commission anywhere from $10,000-$15,000 puts fire into my prospecting.

Number One - I make my initial call to the Expired prospect. I am looking to have a beneficial conversation with nice, sane individuals that may even ask for a callback. Before I let them go, I make sure to secure an email address. I'd say 40% of the time with a new Expired you can retrieve the email.

If I do retrieve the email, I put them in my system to receive a monthly snapshot of homes that sold in their area. Also, I will send them a custom template email introducing myself. Finally, I print this and other contacts out during my prospecting, so at the end of my prospecting session, I can go back to that stack. I send each one a personalized thank you card.

Basically, I say:

> Hello Mr./Mrs. Homeowner,
>
> It was a pleasure speaking with you the other day. You have a wonderful home and I know it will sell quickly. You mentioned you were frustrated with the process. I completely understand. No rush. If you ever need me, I have enclosed my business card. Have a great day.
>
> Sincerely,
> William

I don't write anything fancy. I just put in the card what I'm feeling, and I suggest you do the same. You certainly don't have to use my words, but you can use them as a foundation. Remember, they are getting bombarded with Agents calling and sending letters, so make sure you mention your conversation in the card. It will help them remember you.

Number Two - I normally have things set up to call them again in five or six days. This gives my card plenty of time to arrive. If it's a new Expired, that will hopefully give things time to calm down as far as other Agents calling as well.

Example of my call when I don't have their email:

Mr. Seller, this is William with Super Agent Realty, good morning.

Seller: Good morning. How can I help you?

I was just giving you a quick follow-up call. We spoke a few days ago, and you mentioned to me that you're taking your property off the market and not interested in selling any longer. Is that still the case?

Seller: Yes.

Okay, I can understand that. Did you know in the last three weeks fourteen homes sold, and nine of those homes sold over asking price? Would you like me to send you the information?

Seller: Yes, I would, thank you.

What is your best email address, so I can get that over to you right away?

Seller: hotseller@gmail.com

Okay, thank you. I'll get that over to you right away. In the meantime, I would like to set up a time where I could come over and look at your house. I can show you exactly why it didn't sell and what it takes to get it sold in this market. I'm available today at 5 or would 6:30 be better for your schedule?

Seller: Not now, maybe later.

Okay, I completely understand. I'm just curious were you able to receive my information?

Seller: Oh yes, your thank you card. Thank you!

That's great. Now that I know you have my information, when would be a good time for me to check back in with you?

Seller: Give me two months.

No problem. I'll put it in my calendar, and make sure I stay in touch. Thank you for your time and have a great day.

As you can see, I'm not too pushy about setting the appointment. I'm all about building the relationship, trust, and rapport over time. If I'm not pushy, they will gradually and naturally build some sort of bond with me. In most cases after the transaction, I have more than just a satisfied customer, I have a friend for life. And may I add -- **a Raving Fan!**

In this example, I showed an example of my follow-up script along with asking for the email. Now since I have the email, I will put it into my system, and confirm they received my email the following day.

Also, in this example, he instructed me to give him a call in two months. Generally, you cut that in half; however, if the market has a low inventory, I would stay right on top of them. For example, I would send a card with a picture of their house with a sold banner on the front. Inside, put a screenshot of the neighborhood sales on one side and the ones that sold highest. Three or four properties are enough. On the other side, let them know you just wanted to give them an update and remind them that their home will sell quickly.

If I'm going over your head regarding Send Out Cards and how they work, check out my YouTube video here - http://williejmayenterprises.com/Send_Out_Cards. You can also see more on my website - http://williejmayenterprises.com/recommendations-from-william/

Number Three - After I make the initial steps previously mentioned, I set the potential clients up in my contact management system to receive an automatic call back every other month. I use the same script each time:

Mr. Seller this is William with Super Agent Realty, good morning.

I was just giving you a quick follow-up call. We spoke a while back and you mentioned to me that you're _____. Is that still the case?

Okay, I can understand that. Did you know in the last _____, there were _____ homes that sold, and _____ of those homes sold over asking price? Were you aware that the market is that active?

I would like to pop by and go over three things that will definitely affect the money you put in your pocket when you decide to sell.

First, I would like to look at your home and see what you have to offer the buyers in today's market.

Second, I want to show you a few things that will draw in qualified buyers interested in paying top dollar for your home.

Mr. Seller, would you say that's pretty important for your bottom line?

Seller: Yes!

The third thing is, I'm going to show you why my homes sell, and other Agents' homes do not in this market.

We can get together today at 5 or would 6:30 tomorrow be better for your schedule?

That's it. There's nothing to it. Well, maybe there's a lot to it. You must keep on following up and gauge their motivation. Update the contact record each time you make a contact. Even if they say they're no longer selling, continue to follow up unless they tell you not to. When you follow up, use the FORD technique:

- Family
- Occupation
- Recreation
- Dreams

I will go into more detail on this in a later chapter.

At the end of the conversation, ask for referrals. You know what to say, right?

Who do you know that is looking to buy or sell Real Estate now or in the near future?

As you get more comfortable on the phone, your follow-up and interactions with prospects will improve and increase. Once you get over the initial hurdle of it being uncomfortable, you'll soon start developing a habit of being on the phones interacting with clients and closing deals.

I can just see you now in a few short months taking the steps you've learned from this book to increase your business tenfold. All of it simply because you put forth the work and you embraced the truth: **the money is in the follow-up**.

Just a reminder if you're having trouble with expired objections, check out my other book *Top 10 Expired Objections*. Get a link to it on Amazon from my website - http://williejmayenterprises.com/

For Sale By Owners

I just love Real Estate. You have the Expired Listing that, for whatever reason, expired. You're jumping up and down saying "thank you" to the Real Estate gods for giving you such a great source of business. The icing on the cake is For Sale By Owner or FSBO. These people are the DIY generation who want to do it themselves. They say, "I can save myself the commission. Who needs a Real Estate Agent!?!"

They think it's easy until they try to do it themselves, and then they realize, they need us.

Always remember we are professionals and we should act accordingly. If an FSBO or anyone for that matter, doesn't appreciate your value, move on. There will always be more leads, so don't get stuck on just one client. Have an abundance mindset. To be good at working with Expireds and FSBOs, we have to determine their motivation and if that person is someone with which we are comfortable working.

A lot of Agents try to sell the FSBO on how they cannot sell their house on their own. The truth is they can sell on their own. The real question is: do they want to sell on their own just to see if they can do it, or do they want to sell their home for the most money possible? As a top-producing Real Estate Agent, this is what you need to find out before you go any further.

Identifying the Three Types of FSBOs

FSBOs fall into three categories. (This technique also works for Expireds.) When you reach out to them, it's your job to find out which category fits them best.

1. **Ready and willing to meet** - This group is willing to hear what you have to say and sets an appointment with you.
2. **Not ready; still trying to sell on their own** - These prospects need more time to try to sell on their own. Sooner or later, they will realize doing things on their own is not what it's cracked up to be. With continuous follow-up and persistence, you will have a higher level of conversions than your competition who never follow up.
3. **Trash** - These prospects are not worth following up with. You will encounter a lot of prospects that you have to eliminate for different

reasons. For example, a seller who has no or very little equity to pay commission is out. Other examples include another Agent selling an off-market listing or an investor who isn't willing to cooperate with Agents.

Anytime you are telephone prospecting, the main goal is trying to set an appointment. At first, you will be nervous, unsure of yourself, and doubtful of your abilities. If you practice role-playing and rehearse, you will see your skills get better. The more FSBOs you call, you will see your confidence grow. If I am rusty, say after a vacation or long weekend, I just call without caring what happens during the conversation to get back in verbal shape. You will be pleasantly surprised sometimes to get listings this way.

As your experience grows with calling Expireds or FSBOs, you will get the feel of your prospect. Within thirty to forty-five seconds of the call, you will know which category you can put the prospect in. Understanding and respecting that the FSBO wishes to sell on their own is something we must accept. Everyone wants to save money. The more we stay in contact with them and help them along the way, the more you build layers of rapport with them. That's how we eventually earn their business.

Going After For Sale By Owners

There are different ways to find FSBOs in your area. There are different tools that I use for pulling my FSBOs, such as LANDVOICE, Mojo, and Zillow. Just so we can get to the nitty-gritty, I'm assuming you already have a lead source system that provides you with leads you can prospect. I would suggest using Zillow and Craigslist for FSBOs if you are new to the business and short on funds. For this example, I will be using Zillow.

Zillow is a great way to find FSBOs. Zillow has a feature where you can select a custom radius, and when a new FSBO becomes available, the system will alert you through email. Did I mention this feature is free? You can't beat that!

The way I hunt for my FSBOs is to go into the radius I set up. This area could be a few blocks, a few miles, or even include several cities. I have a fifty-mile radius selected for my prospecting area. When you're selecting your area, you want to make sure that you have a radius that you're comfortable with servicing, but not so big that it's overwhelming.

I have seen many Agents, and I admit I have done it myself, whose eyes were too big for their prospecting ability. They bit off more than they could chew in other words. It's always better to select an area where you can hyper-focus rather than have a larger area where you are spread too thin. If you're spread too thin, you are ineffective, and that is just a waste of time. Remember, we are prospecting for dollars, so we must be efficient with our efforts.

Depending upon your market, you might have a few FSBOs a day, or maybe none. Just keep your eye out, and make sure you set yourself up with the FSBO alert system. You want to be constantly updated when new FSBOs become available in your area.

After a while, you may notice a trend. Some days and weeks, you may have just a few prospects, while others there is a steady wave of activity. Get in the habit of paying attention because, in this business, you can get distracted very easily.

I work FSBOs quite differently than I work Expired Listings. With FSBOs, I use a manual filing system. Yes! It's just what it sounds like: I use paper. When I'm going over my new FSBOs for the day, I can see which ones make good possible leads. I print those when they first come in. It won't be long until I've generated a nice stack of high-quality leads to nurture.

The advantage of a manual filing system is having all the information in front of me at once. The address, how many bedrooms and baths, the square footage, the homeowner's description of the property, the year the home was built, parking, what kind of heating and cooling system are present, and if it has any major upgrades. The most important information on the page is the homeowner's contact information!

Calling the For Sale By Owner

Now you have a stack of FSBOs to call with all their information in front of you. Remember when you call, each one fits into one of three categories: appointment, follow-up, or trash. Let's start dialing!

Hello, I'm calling about the property on 123 Main Street is this the owner.

Seller: Yes.

I see you are advertising the property as a For Sale By Owner. Is this still the case?

Seller: Yes.

OK great, how much will you take for the property?

Seller: $300,000.

That's a good price-point for the market. What's the earliest you would like to have it sold and move by?

Seller: By January.

I can make that happen. You mentioned you're looking to sell the property for $300,000. After you pay off your loan balance and everything is said and done, how much are you looking to net to make that move by January?

Seller: $125,000.

$125,000, that sounds reasonable. If I can get you in the ballpark of $125,000 in your pocket after my fees and escrow fees are paid, would you be okay with that?

Seller: Yes.

I like to meet people in the afternoons or on weekends. Would today at 4 work, or would 5:30 be better?

Seller: 5:30.

I would like to send you my pre-appointment package. It's basically my resume, how I sell homes and my client testimonials. What is your best email address?

Seller: blahblah@gmail.com

Great, thank you! I'll send it over in a few minutes. So, I can be prepared for our meeting this afternoon, I would like to ask you a few quick questions. Do you have a few moments?

Seller: Yes.

You're not going to set an appointment with an FSBO all the time. The above script is a best-case scenario. In most cases, they just want to wait to see if they can do it themselves. You should be completely supportive of that notion.

Why!?!

When they finally realize it's not as easy as it seems, you have been the Agent actively following up with them. You will see how FSBO's start seeking YOU out. They will call you and say, "We tried to do it ourselves and it didn't work out. We want to list our property. When can you come by?"

The main point you need to take away is that you need to communicate with that prospect multiple times to build a rapport that includes trust. Once they have that realization, they will naturally come to you and either request or accept your services. It will take anywhere between eight and fifteen actual conversations with that prospect before you are able to convert them into an appointment.

If you have a typical conversation without setting the appointment, you want to make sure that you try your best to secure the email. That way, you can send them your pre-appointment package. Then the FSBO follow-up process begins.

The For Sale by Owner Follow-Up System

I cannot emphasize enough that you must follow up. Be creative with it. Your follow-up is an essential part of your survival as a Real Estate Agent!

1. Make the initial call. Use the script we went over earlier in this book.
2. Do your best to secure their email addresses.
3. During the conversation, make sure to make notes about your conversation. All the information they provide is valuable like unique attributes of the property, family history, and any unique improvements made to the property. It all qualifies as crucial information. You can refer to these notes when you do your follow up.

4. After prospecting, send the FSBO your pre-appointment package via email.
5. After you send the email, call them and let them know you've just sent them an email with your information, and they can call anytime. If they do not answer, leave a message:

"Good afternoon, this is William with Super Agent Realty. It was my privilege to speak with you earlier. I just wanted to give you a quick call to let you know that I sent over my pre-appointment package via email. If you have any questions, call me anytime at 123-456-7890. Thank you for your time."

It's as simple as that. Always keep your messages short, quick, and to the point.

6. Write a thank you card to the owner saying something like:

"Hello Mr./Mrs. Seller,

It was my privilege speaking to you the other day. You have a wonderful home, and it should sell quickly. You mentioned you had reservations about selling during Q4. Don't worry, this time of year brings serious buyers. If you have any questions, or you are ready to work with me, I have enclosed my business card. Call anytime. Thanks for your time and speak with you soon.

William"

7. Call them the next day to see if they have any questions regarding your pre-appointment package:

"Good morning, Mr./Mrs. Seller, this is William with Super Agent Realty. I was just giving you a quick call to see if you received my pre-appointment package and if you had any questions."

Seller: *Yes, we received it. Thank you, but we don't have any questions at this time.*

No problem! I'm here if you need me. I'm assuming you have a lot of interest in the property. How many showings have you had?

Seller: *None. 2, 6, 15 buyers looking.*

It doesn't matter what they say, respond with this:

"Wow, okay, that's all? You look like you have a wonderful, unique home, Mr./Mrs.

Seller. I know it will generate highly motivated buyers. You mentioned earlier that you were looking to move before the first of the year and that you'd like to sell for $300,000. Is that still the case?

Seller. *Yes.*

"If I were able to generate a buyer with a full-price offer and get you sold in the next thirty to forty-five days, would that work for you?"

Seller. *I'm not looking to list my property at this time. I'm still trying to sell it on my own.*

"I completely understand. Quick question: how long are you going to try to sell it on your own before you decide to work with an Agent?"

Seller. *Two months.*

"Hey, that sounds great, Mr./Mrs. Seller. I'll keep in touch. You have my information. If you need anything, just give me a call.

You might be thinking it's a waste of time following up when they keep on saying that they aren't interested. You must keep in mind that this is one of the building blocks of success. We made another contact with the seller. We confirmed their motivation and when they are looking to sell their property.

Always take the opportunity when it presents itself to set an appointment. Always use their motivation because **the information they give you is invaluable.**

In this example, they're looking to sell before the end of the year. They just need more time before they see how valuable we are to them.

Remember, they said for us to follow up in two months. One of the rules of Real Estate is to cut that time in half. We will be staying in contact with the seller. We will establish our professionalism with consistent follow-up.

8.   Call the seller on day five or six and confirm receipt of your thank you card.

"Hey, Mr./Mrs. Seller. This is William May with Super Agent Realty. How are you doing this morning?"

Seller: *Doing okay. Thank you.*

"The last time we spoke, you said you were looking to move before the first of the year and sell your home for $300,000. Is that still the case?"

Seller: *Yes.*

"Great! I would like to set up a time when I can come over and look at your home. I can show you how I can get your home sold faster and for more money. Would today at 4:30 work, or would 6:00 be better for your schedule?"

Seller: *No. We are still going to try to sell it on our own but thank you for the card.*

"It was my pleasure, anytime. By the way, what method are you using to advertise your home?"

Seller: *Oh, you know, I have a sign out front, I told my family and friends, and I posted it to Facebook. I did pretty much everything you do.*

"Wow. That sounds great. How much activity are you having? Have you had any offers yet?"

Seller: *No offers, but a few people are interested.*

"I would suggest since you know your neighbors, conduct an Open House this weekend. Make some flyers and knock on some doors around your neighborhood and invite seventy-five to a hundred people to your Open House. You have a wonderful home. With a little sweat equity, it will sell itself. I'll call you back in a few days to find out how things went."

Seller: *That's a great idea! Thanks!*

I'm keeping the conversation friendly. After I ask her/him a question, I try to close the appointment. After an initial "no", I offer a valuable suggestion that also lets the owner know he/she is going to have to put in some work.

After I offer the suggestion, I leave things up to the seller. Depending on the day of the week, I may give them another call to see what the date and time of their Open House is set for. Sometimes, I will show up at the Open House toward the end. Usually, the Open House hasn't gone well, and they are happy to see me. I listen to their concerns and feel them out. Again, I try to close the appointment. If they are highly motivated, sometimes I sign the listing right then and there. **All success is continuous persistence.**

9. Follow up your suggestion with a call to see how their neighborhood door knocking went. Hopefully, it wasn't as easy as it looks, and they are ready for you to help them.

10. Continue to follow up with stubborn clients on a weekly basis. I usually contact these prospects weekly on Monday's. If they are doing any kind of prospecting for their home on their own, this usually happens on the weekends. In most cases, they are frustrated with that process. This gives you the perfect opportunity to close the appointment.

11. After a month, if it seems like the prospect is not progressing toward listing with you, put them in a folder labeled "Old FSBO Leads" in your database system.

No matter what type of prospect you are following up with, it's not difficult to stay consistent. Make sure to put prospecting in your calendar as an appointment and follow up!

For Sale by Owner Open Houses

You're probably asking yourself, "William, what do you mean by For Sale By Owner Open Houses? Are we going to help them with the Open House and hold their hands? Are we going to give them the information they need to conduct their own Open House?"

When I first heard this strategy, I had a lot of questions of my own. This is not your typical Open House. This is a focused Open House that is targeted for sellers. Yes, seller! I'm not that interested in buyers. We are looking for sellers in the community who are thinking about selling and want to work with an Agent that's going to get the job done.

Let's say that you reach an agreement with an FSBO on the terms and conditions of helping them with their Open House. There's a ton of different ways to reach an agreement regarding commission when finding a buyer. We are going to be focusing on securing homeowners who want to list now, or in the near future.

If you don't know, I'm working in Southern California. In every state, there are different laws and regulations on how you conduct your Real Estate business. You would have to check with your own Board of Realtors in your state for guidelines on how to work out an agreement with the homeowner in this situation.

Also, make sure that you are completely transparent with any buyers or potential sellers. Let them know that this is not your listing, and you're just cooperating with the homeowner and assisting them with an Open House. Always be clear, transparent, and honest about your communication with potential clients, so there will be no misunderstandings at any point!

I stress this especially because California is the land of the lawsuit. Someone will sue you for a hangnail claiming it's your fault. Always take precautions in your business to avoid any possible confusion.

Successful Open House Game Plan

Understand we have a mission on locating, targeting, and acquiring homeowners that are thinking about selling now or in the near future. Twenty-five percent of your traffic going through an Open House are sellers thinking about selling their home. Essentially, you have multiple eyes on you: the FSBO seller, the buyers, and most of all, your potential neighborhood seller leads.

The FSBO is looking closely at your work performance and professionalism during the Open House. At the same time, they are also judging you to see how you do an Open House differently from the one they conducted, and if all went as planned. They listened to your suggestion to have their own Open House. Most likely, a civilian's Open House won't have the same effect as that of a trained, professional, Real Estate Agent.

With your Real Estate knowledge and training, your Open House will be like night and day as far as the results. They should be impressed and see the value in hiring you as their Agent to get their home sold.

To show the FSBO seller that we're the best choice for getting their home sold, we must level-up our game plan; 10x our activities. This way, if there's any chance of them hiring us they will see our value during this Open House process.

For the best results, I would suggest planning the Open House two weeks in advance. This will give you ample time to get ready. Most sellers want things done yesterday, and this is the same with FSBO sellers. In most cases, you will only have a week or so to work with, so make sure to use your time efficiently.

Plan the Open House for a Saturday or Sunday if possible. Having a well-planned Open House over a weekend will produce the best results.

The home must be show ready! Let the seller know that for best results, the home must be ready to show before the Open House. This ensures the home is shown in its best possible shape, so you get the highest possible offers. Present them with an Open House checklist like the following:

☐ Declutter the entire home
☐ Clean the home or have it professionally cleaned
☐ Power wash the exterior and driveways
☐ Mow, touch up landscaping
☐ Trim trees and shrubs
☐ Clean the gutters
☐ If a pool or hot tub are present, make sure they are fresh and clean
☐ Clean out the garage if possible
☐ Remove all unnecessary vehicles from the property

These are just a few suggestions off my own Open House checklist. Use your own judgment and make sure the property presents itself in the best light possible.

Get the word out! Getting the word out can take several different forms. At the minimum, make sure you have a full week before your Open House. Let's assume today is Monday and your Open House starts on Saturday. The first thing we need to do is email your database about the upcoming Open House. If you are social media savvy, post to your accounts about the Open House. I recommend making three separate posts on each platform: one on Monday, another on Wednesday, and the last on Friday. Post a reminder about the Open House and let them know to bring their checkbooks!

If you use a service like MyRealEstateTools.com, CoreFact.com, or another postcard service, consider targeting between one hundred and five hundred homes around the property and send them a postcard. Only do this if you can afford it. Don't ever spend your last dime on advertising thinking it will save you. I have been there, done that, and absolutely nothing happened. Trust me, only use marketing when you're in a good financial position to do so.

Pick up the phone! Call your database, friends, and family. Let them know you have an Open House coming up this weekend. Of course, you already emailed them, but the open rate on emails is atrocious.

It's time to circle-prospect, better known as cold calling. You need to contact one hundred to five hundred homeowners in the area and let them know the property is for sale. You're going all out.

You're going to be busy working on those calls but don't get too busy to know the tell-tale sign of interest. If they are asking questions like how much the property is, how many bedrooms, or how many bathrooms, you are probably talking to a homeowner who is thinking about selling.

They probably won't admit it, but rest assured, they are thinking about it. One day, they're going to have that itch, and you need to keep in touch, so you can scratch it!

Keep notes, dig in, get more information! Ask questions like how long they have lived in the home, does it have major upgrades, how old is the roof, if they move, where are they looking to live? You know what you're doing. Plant that seed! When you start door knocking, you're going to make a special note to make sure you contact that homeowner. You want that **face to face, belly to belly**, conversation!

I highly suggest using a dialing system to auto-dial your calls for you. I use the Mojo Dialer from MojoSells - http://williejmayenterprises.com/recommendations-from-william/. Something like this will make short work on the one hundred to five hundred calls you need to make. Hand-dialing will take you a long while, so if you have the means, a dialer will pay for itself in short order. That is *if* **you make the calls!**

Go through the neighborhood twice: once at the beginning of the week, and again at the end. Your goal is to keep the Open House fresh in everyone's minds.

Hit those doors! Okay, ladies and gentlemen, it's time to roll up your sleeves and put on some comfortable shoes. We are going door-to-door! Depending upon how experienced you are with door knocking, I suggest you go through the neighborhood twice. Yes, all one hundred to five hundred homes.

It usually takes me about an hour and a half to do a hundred homes which depends greatly on how many people I talk to. I would suggest not doing more than two hundred houses in a day, especially if you're not in good shape. To hit a high quantity of doors, you must be experienced and in shape.

Choose the number of houses you will visit based on your skill level and physical condition. If you are new to door knocking and not in shape, wait until Friday and do thirty, fifty, or seventy-five homes. Hit a spot where you feel comfortable and set a goal. If you start feeling fatigued, stop and conserve your energy for the main event, your Open House!

Handouts! Okay, Agents, when you're out there in the field knocking on those doors, make sure you are giving homeowners a high-quality product. Do not give them a cheap business card or a plain black and white flyer. Make sure that whatever you're handing out is high quality. Remember, you want them to hire you and trust you with their most important asset. That is not going to happen with a black and white flyer.

Really?

I would slam the door in your face!

Seriously, when you meet these homeowners, you are basically applying for the job of representing them in the most expensive transaction they're ever going to make, so make sure you have a quality flyer. It needs to be well-designed, have a great description, and outstanding photos.

You want this flyer to be printed on high-gloss, 100-pound paper. One side should have the information about the property, and the other side should offer them something of value such as an instant home evaluation, your contact information, and offer to answer any questions they may have. Make it catchy and include a call to action. They will either call you or go to your website.

Once you identify that they have the interest and are thinking about selling their property, they stay on your radar until they list, die, or tell you to stop contacting them. We will talk about this more when we discuss your database.

When I pass out flyers, I wrap them around a notepad. They might keep the flyer, but even if they toss it, my notepad will become part of the family. It will play Gin Rummy, Dominoes, or go along to the supermarket. My notepads even go to church and help take notes on the Sunday service. **Notepads have stickability.**

I can't tell you how many times I've been door-knocking in my farm area and had someone chase me down for another notepad or call me and request another one. There's a little secret out there that not too many coaches will tell you: **notepads are the secret weapon on winning a farm area.**

Notepads are a tool to help you stay in front of the client. If you're financially strapped and you can't purchase flyers, check with your Lender to see if you can work out a partnership where they cover the flyers on their end. Be sure and check with your brokerage first to ensure you are not breaking any rules or regulations.

Check on the property the day before the Open House. While you are running around like a crazy person, stop by the property to make sure the Open House checklist has been completed and everything is to your liking.

Game on! Open House Day! You should be excited. Your hard work and determination will show today. Just a few more housekeeping details to make sure the day goes off without a hitch.

Expect a full house. Depending upon the amount of traffic you are expecting, you should have a two-person team working your Open House. I would suggest that the team be made up of you and a Lender. That way you can transform the Open House into a one-stop-shop. Having a Lender will help you manage the potential clients coming in and help you screen potential buyers that are pre-qualified, as well as those who are not.

This is completely up to you, but I think it's a good idea to set up an agreement with a good Buyer's Agent that will agree to pay you a 25% referral fee for any buyers you refer and they close escrow with. That percentage is just an example, it can be any percentage the two of you can agree on. Our main goal is to acquire listings, FSBO listings, and listings from the community.

A few hours before the event, put up fifteen to thirty signs around the neighborhood advertising your Open House. There are companies you can hire to do this for you, or you can have your Buyer's Agent to take care of the job. Have a lot of signs everywhere. This is a 10x Open House, it's MEGA! Whatever you call it, if you're serious about producing listings for your business, we are stepping up our game. This system can be used for any Open House and it will generate listings and passive referral income from the Buyer's Agent.

Arrive at the Open House a minimum of an hour before it begins. This will give you plenty of time should anything unexpected pop up.

Picture it: You have signs all over the neighborhood with the tall banners, signs, and flags out front. Just before the Open House begins, BBQ Pete's smoking, joking, catering truck pulls up and starts blowing barbecue smoke all over the neighborhood. You invited all the neighbors over for free barbecue and to check out the Open House.

You don't have to do the catering truck, but in Los Angeles, they're not that expensive. There are so many options with the trucks. Some are health food, Mexican, Italian, and the list goes on. If you can imagine it, there's probably a catering truck for it. You can also go the traditional route, and offer a simple spread of wine, cheese, cookies, or whatever you are comfortable with.

Dress the part! Dress to impress, ladies and gentlemen. No white shirts and flip flops. You are directly paid on your level of professionalism including your attire, so look and present yourself professionally. Don't go to late-night parties the night before. In fact, go to bed early so you are on the very top of your game.

Sign them in! Have a sign-in sheet (or an iPad) at the door so you can grab the information of these potential clients as they come in. Let them know that once they sign in and their information is verified, you will give them a voucher for the catering truck. You will have some who don't want to sign in no matter what. Let them know that the homeowner has requested that everyone sign in for safety reasons. If they are represented by an Agent, receiving the Agent's business card will suffice for sign-in for me, but it's up to you how you want to handle that.

TIP: Always be professional. Don't give buyers who come in with an Agent the cold shoulder. Answer all their questions and be sure to give them vouchers for the catering truck especially. You are running a small business here, and if you treat potential clients unprofessionally, that will get around through the grapevine. Even though you're in competition with other Agents in your area, you should always help them out. Set the example.

Once things are in full swing, and you're seeing some traction, that is the perfect time to pull out your phone and do a Facebook Live video with an app called Live Leap - http://williejmayenterprises.com/recommendations-from-william/. This app syndicates your Facebook Live to your own Page, Group, and other places on Facebook you want to share the video. Send the video to the seller's Timeline! All their friends and family will see the Mega Open House you've put together and they will be crazy not to hire you. Look at the magnitude of work you've put in to show them that you are different!

Don't sit down! During this event, you must interact with people. If people are coming up the house, go out and greet them! This is not your typical Open House; we are on the hunt for sellers! Be familiar with the area, the types of homes in the area, the local school district, what is the highest-priced home that sold in the neighborhood. Do your homework, so when you meet those potential sellers, they will see you as an authority on the neighborhood even if they've never seen you before. This will help you establish a connection with them.

Here's a script for interacting with potential sellers:

With confidence:

Good afternoon! Welcome to our Open House today. My name is William May. What's yours?

Potential Seller: Mr./Mrs. Joe Buyer/Mr./Mrs. Joe Seller.

Nice to meet you, [insert name here]. I know you probably have a few questions about the house and neighborhood, so let me tell you about the house, and maybe I can answer some of the other questions you have.

This is a Craftsman-style home with an open floor plan. There are four bedrooms with two and a half baths. There is a little over 2,100 square feet of living space with a 10,000-square foot lot. The home has central air and heating. It was built in 1997.

Since then, the home has had only one owner. It is in a very prestigious neighborhood called Circle Hills Estates. If you don't mind me asking, how did you hear about the Open House?

If you noticed from the script, I do several things here that you should take note of. Seriously, if you have this book, feel free to scribble in the margins. If you are listening on Audible or reading the eBook, make sure you're taking notes in a way that's comfortable for you.

I am interacting with a potential client with confidence and authority. I have demonstrated my market knowledge of the neighborhood. I have done my homework. You do not want to be one of those Agents when someone asks one of the following questions and you can't answer:

1. How old is the roof?
2. Any major upgrades?
3. What are the schools like?
4. What school district is this?

"I don't know" is a bad answer that will not earn you any business. It can take a bit of practice, but if you put the time in, you will become better and better at it. You will be scared and nervous at first, but the more you do it, the better you will become.

If you are speaking with buyers, they will see that you know what you are talking about. With the information you've initially provided, you have already answered the most common buyer questions. If you are speaking with a seller, they will already know most of the answers, but this is a great opportunity to impress them when they see you know your stuff.

If they are thinking about selling, they are going to naturally gravitate toward you because you are knowledgeable. That's exactly what we want! We want to win over sellers.

Their answer to your question is very important. If they say they learned about the Open House through your signs, then you know the number of signs you put out is good. If they say the Internet, that is good because it means your social media, Craigslist post, or Zillow advertisements regarding your Open House are working well. If they say they received your personal invitation through your door-knocking campaign, then you can take that as a slam dunk. They know you mean business and you are producing results. Your job, no matter what kind of prospect they are, is to qualify them and see how you can help.

On the side note: You must consider that your Open House signs, banners, flags, and Mr. Pete's BBQ catering truck is enhancing your Open House success rate exponentially. You're using their senses to entice them. Think about that for a second. All your Open House signs and the smell of barbecue in the air is like leading a mouse to cheese. It looks like a party and the curiosity is thick. It makes people want to pull up and check out the Open House. That is exactly why this works.

You don't have to go to this level, but you get the idea. If you've been in the business for any length of time, you know that Open Houses generally do not sell homes. The Agent activity sells the house. After everything has been said and done, your Buyer's Agent picks up the signs, your Lender closes shop for the day with a ton of leads you both generated.

The seller will inevitably say, "This was a long day, we had a lot of traffic, but I didn't get an offer on my home."

Here is what you say to that:

"Mr./Mrs. Seller, you see how I work. If you want to get your home sold, I could come back tomorrow with my eighteen-point marketing plan and show you exactly how I can get your home sold for top dollar while doing all the work for you. Would tomorrow at 1:00 work, or would 2:00 be better for your schedule?"

After the Open House, you should have generated a good quantity of leads. Have your Lender and the Buyer's Agent work with the buyer leads. As a precaution, remind them to contact those leads that night or the following day to follow up so they do not forget you. Make sure they follow up!

At the same time, some of those leads were sellers who might need to sell and then purchase another home soon, so make sure you nurture those leads in your database. Contact them the same day or the following day. Thank them for taking the time to come out and see the Open House. Let them know that if there's anything they need; they can give you a call anytime. Send them a thank you card and follow up with them according to their motivation to sell.

Remember, there are no guarantees with anything I teach in this book, but with this strategy, it's highly possible to generate very good buyer and seller leads. Try it out and let me know about your experience by emailing me at william@williejmayenterprises.com.

Past Clients, SOI, and Your Database

One of the best parts of having a successful business in Real Estate is having a referral-based business. People who know you, like you and trust you. Your friends, family, neighbors, mechanic, plumber, doctor, lawyer, pastor, and babysitter; these people are your raving fans. They like you, care about you, and if you have that award-winning personality, they may even love you!

They are going to refer business to you. It's not a coincidence when you listen to interviews by top producers. One of the main sources of their business is referrals. Have you asked yourself why that is? Let me give you something to think about to put it into perspective. Have you ever referred somebody to your place of work? Has someone ever referred you to theirs simply because they cared about you and your well-being?

It's the same with Real Estate. If your friends, family, and past clients care about you and your business, they're going to do whatever they can to support you and your business. That's why so many Agents are attracted to a referral-based business. To have a successful, referral-based business, you must make contact with your past clients, SOI, and your database.

To simplify the system and make it easy for you, we are just going to integrate all three forms of clients into one. We'll just call it, you guessed it, your database! Let's get to work.

Creating Your Database

Just in case you're a brand-new Agent or an Agent that has never worked your database, I'll show you how to build your database from the ground up. Let's start by using your cell phone. How many contacts do you have in your phone? A hundred? Five hundred? A thousand? Whatever the number, that is a good place to start. You need a good contact management system inside a customer relations manager or CRM to manage your contacts with ease.

In my last book, *Top 10 Expired Objections*, I mentioned that I use two CRMs:

- Mojo Dialer
- Contactually

You can find out more about both on my website –
http://williejmayenterprises.com/recommendations-from-william/.

I still use both, but for this chapter, I going to focus on Contactually.

Full disclosure: as of this writing, I do not get paid from this company. I truly
believe this CRM is a good and easy way to keep in constant contact with your
database. Contactually also includes an accountability feature that I really appreciate.

Integrating your contacts into Contactually is very easy and seamless. For
example, if you have Gmail, it's as easy as logging into your Gmail account in the
Contactually system and letting it import all your contacts. Voila! One of the best
features that I love about Contactually is that it updates the contact information each
time you email them, send a text message, or call them. All your communication is
visible in the database. Did I mention that I love this feature?

Contactually has so many systems and resources, there is no way I can cover
them all, but once you import your contacts, there is a cool game where you sort all
your contacts into different buckets. The game is called the Bucket Game. You can
customize each bucket with a name, frequency, and to-do list. For example, you
might have one where contacts in that bucket start an 8x8 system that you created.

Also, I have trouble with names sometimes, and Contactually has an option
where you can include a picture of your contact in their profile. This is so helpful to
me because it helps me remember that contact on a deeper level. When I call them, I
can remember what they look like.

If you're not comfortable with any of the multiple line dialers out there, I have a
solution for you: Kixie.

It's a wonderful program that's not that expensive. You can click to call your
clients, and it integrates seamlessly with Contactually. It also integrates with several
other database systems. You can make and receive calls, have your calls recorded,
text message, drop pre-recorded voicemails, and it automatically updates your
database with a log and more.

If you're interested and would like to learn more, email Kixie at hello@kixie.com.
In the subject line, type: William May Referral. Simply let them know you were
referred by me. You will receive a fourteen-day trial with no credit card required. See
a video of it in action - **https://www.youtube.com/watch?v=XX2Hoo_DBsQ.**

With Kixie or without, Contactually's system is very robust. I would suggest you go to the website and check out their tutorials. You will fall in love with it. If this is not your cup of tea, the systems I'm going to share with you can be used with any other contact management system that you feel comfortable with.

Who do we put in our database? We want to make sure that we get everybody we know into our new database. This list includes immediate and extended family, friends, church, neighborhood watch, social groups like Facebook, current and past clients, your vendor list, mechanic, doctor, lawyer, escrow officer, and so on. Understand this is going to be the lifeblood of your business. Remember if they have a pulse and they like you, they go in your database.

Vendor List

Make sure you create a vendors list. A vendor list is essential to your business and the relationship that you build with your clients. Life happens so it is always best to be prepared. If you have a good electrician, plumber, handyman, or painter that you can refer your clients to, it will make you look like a hero. When you help your clients out of a situation, that pays dividends in the long run.

Their Ideal Information

Obviously, we want to pack as much information in their profile as possible including, but not limited to: first and last name, relationship, address, email, telephone number, description of your relationship, birthday, anniversaries, kids, and their pet's favorite food. I'm not saying go as far as getting their blood type, but if you can add it into your database, do it.

You will not be able to get all this valuable information on the first call. You will retrieve it through a series of interactions with your client by listening. The more you listen, the more rapport and trust you build with your contacts. It's a continuous exercise, at least for me, not to talk so much during the conversation. I must remember to listen 80% of the time and speak 20% of the time. That is when opportunities present themselves.

For example, you have a conversation with a client, and they mention their son's sixteenth birthday in June which is a few months away. This gives you the perfect opportunity to send a birthday card with some sort of gift card inside. You mail that off a week and a half before June, and you follow up with them in the first part of June to see if they received your birthday card. You give them a call, that's if they don't call you first. Little steps like these, help build an unbreakable rapport with your clients that no other Agent can compete with.

If you want to step up your game to the next level I suggest you use Send Out Cards. Send Out Cards is very easy to use. You can customize gift cards and greeting cards. You can also send all sorts of gifts. Check out my interview with Gayle Zientek, the Send Out Card Queen - https://youtu.be/eHW5XxDdzpQ

In this interview, we go deep into showing you how to use the system and how to use it to follow up. If you would like to get signed up.

check out this link - http://williejmayenterprises.com/sendoutcards.

The FORD Technique

One of the best passive ways to get most of all the information you need from your client is to use the FORD technique in regular conversation. This is a great technique if you are nervous about calling your past clients or sphere of influence. It gives you a system to start and continue a conversation where if you did not use this technique, you would just be holding the phone looking silly. No one likes having those awkward conversations.

That's why I like to use the FORD technique so much. Before I used this technique, I was so scared about picking up the phone. I always had to do something other than having a conversation with someone because I was so scared. I was suffering from **avoidance behavior;** I was doing busy work instead of prospecting.

The thing is, the more I picked up the phone, and talked to people while practicing the FORD technique, the more comfortable I became on the phone. The effects spilled over into my personal interactions as well with family, friends, and just starting conversations with people.

Since I know my scripts and I use the FORD technique, it has helped with my cold calling exponentially. In the first six months of 2017, I called more than 100,000 numbers and talked to 6,000 people. You cannot reach that level if you are scared to talk to people.

You have heard this many times before, and I never believed it myself, "If I can do it, you can definitely do it!"

I believe now because I'm not crippled by not knowing what to say. I always know what to say. I take time to practice and rehearse, and because of this simple technique, so can you!

The Ford Technique is outlined as follows:

Family
Occupation
Recreation
Dreams

F Stands for Family

Family is always a great topic of discussion. Who doesn't want to talk about their family? If you are talking to your clients, they love talking about their kids. Little Johnny just made it into Little League, their daughter, Jessica, just got a scholarship to a prestigious college, or their grandkids are growing up like little weeds. People are proud of their kids.

If you put your mind to it, there are a hundred and one topics of discussion, but always remember to keep the conversation light, simple, and easy. Never ask personal questions or questions regarding gossip. Never go down the rabbit hole of negativity. Always focus on the positives.

Here are a few examples you can ask regarding their family:

1. How long has your family been living in this neighborhood?
2. Are you originally from Houston, Texas?
3. How did you meet your wife?
4. How is your family?
5. How are your children?
6. What's your dog's name? (Yes, of course, dogs are family too!)

O Stands for Occupation

Talking about their occupation can be interesting. Your clients can either have a job or a career. In any case, they probably know a lot about the field they work in. This makes this topic of discussion very interesting because many times I've learned things about a career I did not know. At the same time, it lets your clients feel that you truly are interested in them, their career, and their well-being.

Here are a few examples you can ask regarding their occupation:

1. What attracted you to your present career?
2. What do you like most about your career?
3. How long have you been in your present career?
4. Do you have family and friends that are interested in your career?

TIP: Do not ask questions about money or salary. The only exception to the rule with this is if they're able to buy a property. The best practice is to have your preferred Lender handle this discussion.

R Stands for Recreation

Recreation could be a wide range of things such as sports, movies, or vacations. Dig in and see what kind of fun activities they like to get involved in or use to unwind. Maybe they like going to the movies during the weekends with the kids. Maybe after a hard day's work, they like to relax by reading a good book. When you find similarities between what you like and what your clients like, this helps the conversation and the bonding process.

Here are a few examples you can ask regarding recreation:

1. Have any vacation plans in the near future?
2. What do you do for fun?
3. How is your favorite sports team doing?
4. What is your favorite book?
5. Have you seen any good movies lately?

If you find you and your client have similar interests, expound on that, and take notes for future conversations.

D Stands for Dreams

I always like talking to people about their dreams. Their dreams can be anything from starting a new business to seeing their children graduate from college. It could even be a simple weight loss goal before their 20th reunion. You really find out about a person on a deeper level when they share what their main goals in life are. When you take interest in what they care about and support them, believe me, this means the world to them.

Here are a few examples you can ask regarding their dreams:

1. If money was no object, where in the world would you travel to?
2. You said you were going to go back to school, what would you take up?

3. Have you ever thought about writing a book, and if so, what about?
4. When you retire what are your plans? Will you travel the world or maybe a road trip?
5. Where is the most exotic place you ever traveled, and would you do it again?

As I said before, the more you communicate with people and use the FORD technique, the better communicator you become. Every time you're touching your database, make sure that you have a notepad or scratchpad, so you can take notes. Later, put those notes in your database.

Remember, let them talk 80% of the time while you only talk 20% of the time. You should mostly be asking questions. Listen, learn, and take notes. Always smile when you talk to your clients. It's crazy but they can hear your smile through the phone and that passes on your positive energy. I hope I'm not the only one that can hear somebody smiling over the phone.

Your Year-Round Follow-Up Plan

We are going to start off with one hundred contacts in your database. More is better, but for this example, we are going to start with a hundred for the sake of easy math. These contacts are a mixture of past clients, a sphere of influence, and vendors. Like I said before, if they have a pulse and they like you, then they should be in your database.

The point of staying in contact with everyone is so you always stay in the front of their mind when they, or someone they know, needs any sort of Real Estate service.

The 5-Step System

This 5-step system is one you need to use on a continuous basis. I dare you to find any top-producing Agent that bases their business on referrals. They will confirm that they stay in front of their database consistently. This is proven with Realtors across the country, day in and day out.

The bonus of working with your database is dealing with people that care about you, like you, trust you, are past clients, and people with whom you work. The conversations flow more freely and there's no anxiety when you pick up the phone to call them because you know what to say.

Even if it's been a while since you spoke with them, it's not a big deal because you are going to implement this follow-up system and get back in touch with the people who matter most: your database.

Email

Send out an email of pertinent information to your database bi-weekly. That's around twenty-six emails per year.

One tool I use is Google Alerts - https://www.google.com/alerts. I have it set up so I get an update once a week on the California Real Estate market. On the second Sunday of each month, I do a Bomb Bomb video speaking on Real Estate news that I have received from Google Alerts, or some other topic that I think would interest my clients.

With Bomb Bomb - http://williejmayenterprises.com/recommendations-from-william/ - I can schedule my videos for release on Monday morning to my database.

Making and syndicating the videos only takes me a few minutes. The most effective thing about this method is to be consistent. Several of my clients have told me that they look forward to my video reports.

I use Corefact - http://williejmayenterprises.com/recommendations-from-william/ - the last week of the month to send everyone a neighborhood update with homes that recently sold during that month. I get notified when they open the attachment. Wouldn't you like to get notified each time someone is curious about the value of their home? I would!

The best thing about sending out a localized market update is reaching homeowners who are on the fence about selling. When they receive your market update, it reminds them that they have another mortgage payment in a few days. The information you send might be just enough to knock them off that fence and list with you. **Follow-up is the key to success!**

There are many different email companies out there. Experiment and see which one works best for you.

Snail Mail

I love to send out a postcard once a month to my clients. I use My Real Estate Tools - http://williejmayenterprises.com/recommendations-from-william/ - and one of their products that I enjoy is the monthly postcards. I put my database on a campaign and have never had a problem with their system. The monthly postcard campaign is designed to stay in front of your database with your branding, your face, and your business. I've never had to worry about breaking the bank with My Real Estate Tools as they are very affordable.

You can also use Send Out Cards and send them a custom card. Whatever you decide to use, the goal is to be the Agent they mention any time they think of Real Estate services.

Phone Calls

Set your contact management system to call your database every sixty days. When we cover the fourth quarter follow-up plan, you will up your game for keeping in touch with your clients.

Always have the mindset that these are easy calls to make. Don't let the drunken monkey tell you anything different even if you haven't spoken to someone in a few years. You are calling them now, and that's all that matters.

Here's a quick script for calling someone you haven't talked to in a long time:

Hello, Mr./Mrs. Past Client. It's amazing how time flies, how have you been? Wow, that's wonderful. How is the family?

That's amazing how kids grow these days. How's everything at work?

Congratulations on your promotion! The last time we spoke, you said you were working on the backyard to create a relaxation area. How is that coming along?

Sounds wonderful! I'm going to have to pop by one day soon. Do you have any vacation plans in the near future?

Mr./Mrs. Past Client, it's always a privilege talking to you. If you ever need me, give me a call. Have a great day.

Always take notes when you have a conversation. This is useful for your follow-up calls. Send them a thank you card that same day. If you like Send Out Cards, this is the perfect situation to send out a custom card congratulating them on their promotion or whatever is going on in life.

If you are friends on Facebook, you can always take a picture from their Timeline to further customize your card. For example, say they got a new puppy, you can send out a card saying, "It was good speaking with you the other day. Congratulations on your new family member. Have a great day, and I'll speak with you soon."

All these contacts, or touches and interactions, are building up like a compound effect. You are slowly building a powerhouse of referrals one client at a time.

Pop By

I love to pop by my client's homes. You should go by once every three months. Don't stay long and bring something of value like a notepad, market update, or simple gift. If you need ideas, visit Brian Buffini's website - https://www.buffiniandcompany.com/pbt.htm. He has a ton of pop-by gift ideas.

There is nothing like a belly-to-belly, face-to-face in Real Estate. If you're taking the time to show up at the front door just to check in because you're in the neighborhood, that puts you in a different category of relationship.

For example, I was knocking on doors in my farm area, passing out my newsletter and notepads, when I came across a homeowner who asked me if I knew a good plumber. I do have a couple I deal with, so I told them I could get them the info in an hour or so. I asked for their best phone number, and once I received it, I asked for their email as well. I told the homeowner that I had a list of vendors that I work with that includes electricians, plumbers, and handymen. I asked if that would be a list of value to her, and she said, "Yes!"

So, I sent her the information via email and called to verify that she received it. Then, I put her in my database just as I'm telling you to do. To make a long story short, she already had a family Realtor that sold her a home, but because I was there for her, I follow up and pop by at least once a quarter, I am her Real Estate Agent of choice now. I built a relationship over time, and face-to-face is the best way to accomplish that.

This is an easy system, but most Agents have a hard time staying with it. What I have found most effective for me is that I check my calendar the Sunday night before my week starts. Let's say I have five pop-bys for that week. I can knock that out early Saturday morning when most people are home.

I use an app called Road Warrior Route Planner - https://roadwarriorllc.com on my phone. It is amazing! I have been in transportation for over twenty-five years. I owned my own school bus company, and I must say this app is one of the best and simplest to use in my opinion. It works for Android or iOS. You just input all your addresses that you are going to hit that day, tap **Optimize**, and in a few short seconds, it plans out your route synced with your phone's GPS. By default, it plans the shortest possible route. It's a huge time-saver.

Special Dates

When we work in our database, we are going to:

1. Email them bi-weekly.
2. Send them snail mail once per month.
3. Call them every other month. If they don't answer, leave a message.

4. Every three months you need to grace your database with your presence.

So that's four, what is the fifth system?

Special dates.

Every client in your database should have special dates for their birthday, their children's birthdays, wedding anniversaries, the anniversary of their home purchase, and any other date of significance. They should all be on your calendar.

For example, let's say you have a client who purchases a home. You do an active follow-up with that client according to this system. They know you, they like you, they trust you, and they love you because you've stayed in contact with them. When most Agents would have called it "job done", you're still in the game!

It is the month of the anniversary of the purchase of their home, so you send them an updated CMA on their property, a custom anniversary card from Send Out Cards, and a handwritten letter. Depending upon your schedule, drop by their home within a few days of their anniversary or on the day of, and congratulate them. This will turn your database clients into raving fans. When it comes time for them to sell their home, they will come to you because you demonstrated your value to them consistently and persistently.

This is just one example of custom dates. This might sound crazy, but your database is a living, breathing system that needs constant attention because it is the life source of your business. If you don't take care of your database, it will die, and then your business will die. Without it, you can't generate new business. If your business is stagnant or dying, it is because you have not been working your database, or worse, you don't have a database.

The good news is, if you have a database, you can begin working it today! If you don't have one, you can start building one right now! Don't wait. If you are interested in your financial future, I suggest that you start working on your database as soon as possible.

Do You Have a Real Estate Business Exit Strategy?

Remember Neil's quote?

"90% of what's wrong in your life today can be cured by Massive prospecting."

This is my little spin on his famous quote:

"90% of what's wrong in your life today.... Can be cured by MASSIVE Prospecting and PASSIVE INCOME" - William J. May

I'm going to warn you right now this is probably one of the most important chapters in this book. I want you to really open your mind and see where you want to be in the next few years because most people do not have a business plan not to mention an exit strategy for their Financial Freedom.

Where do you see yourself three, five, or ten years from now? Do you have an exit strategy? There's a saying in real estate: "we're only as good as our last close deal." In a lot of ways, we're like that earned income employee working 9 to 5 working paycheck to paycheck. The difference in our world is its commission check to commission check.

My father was a Marine and he always taught me to analyze your situation. Always look at the worst-case scenario and prepare for it. My father said, "If you take the steps to prepare yourself for the worst-case scenario, no matter what happens, you'll be in a better place than if you did nothing at all. So, let me ask you, what would happen to your business if you got hurt, or the economy crashed? Would you be prepared financially?

I hope you understand these are very serious, deep questions. I want you to really take this seriously. Thinking about these questions, I want you to analyze your life and business goals. Take my father's advice and look at the worst-case scenario that can happen to your business and prepare to overcome those obstacles.

I'm not a financial advisor but, as a fellow real estate agent, you should know where I'm coming from when I say we are in an exciting, highly profitable business. Real Estate Sales! We're in the business where we can make more money than doctors, lawyers and even the President of the United States. Why not take advantage of our position in real estate to build our business beyond real estate sales and into a business of passive income.

You look on YouTube, Instagram, and some of these other social media sites and you'll see some Superstar Real Estate Agents Driving Lamborghinis and living in multimillion-dollar houses claiming that they and their team, are doing 50 to 100 deals a year. You also have these real estate trainers or gurus teaching you if you're not doing so many deals a year there's something wrong with you and you need to buy their course or purchase a one-on-one training.

I'll be the first to tell you I'm not one of those real estate agents that drives a Lamborghini or lives in a big mansion. I'm just like you and most other agents trying to work hard and support my family. If you're a real estate agent, you are closing a decent amount of deals per year. and you're happy with it, then, in my opinion, you're a successful agent. The point of this chapter is setting you up with your exit strategy. Before we get into that, let me explain my opinion of the evolution of a successful real estate agent.

Every agent you know or have known is in one of four Real Estate agent categories. The New agent, the seasoned agent, the investor agent, and the passive income agent. These categories I have branded as "The evolution of a successful real estate agent." My goal is to have you recognize which category you fit into and move up to the final category: The Passive Income Agent.

They may not be self-explanatory so let me explain the different types of Agents.

- **The New Agent:** As the title suggests, they are a new agent, new in the business, they're green. They are eager to learn the business and succeed, but so many times they realize how hard the business really is, and end up quitting or worse, they never take the extra steps.
- **The Seasoned Agent:** The seasoned agent has been in the business for a certain amount of time and knows the business. Nine times out of ten, his or her business is doing pretty well or at least decent. They have a work schedule and a prospecting plan that works for them and their business.

  Unfortunately, they're at the mercy of the economy and the housing market so they just stay on the hamster wheel of real estate sales with no real plan for retirement or even an exit strategy. In most cases, not all.

- **The Investor Agent:** Is doing pretty well with their Real estate business and investing their capital either in flipping properties or other forms of Investments.
- **The Passive Income Agent:** Now we're getting into the nitty-gritty! Obtaining passive income should be every real estate agents' goal. Having enough passive income from your rental properties to pay off all of your business and living expenses; hence, The Passive Income Agent!

To become a Passive Income Agent, you're going to have to know that this is not going to be done overnight. This is a multi-year process depending on your income, your goals, and your mindset.

I have to admit I am not at this level as of yet, but it feels good to be on my way. I own my own home and my wife and I have an income property that is our foundation to our real estate empire. I have big dreams and goals. When you're reading this book and I'm talking about a real estate exit strategy, this is exactly what I mean: building a real estate empire on investment properties where you have passive income that pays your business and living expenses.

I listen to a lot of audiobooks and one day I was listening to Robert Kiyosaki's *Rich Dad Poor Dad*. After that, I could not get enough of Mr. Kiyosaki's information. I was hooked. Now if you add Robert Kiyosaki's teachings, what my father taught me about preparing yourself for worst-case scenarios, and sprinkle in a little bit of Brandon Turner and David Greene from Bigger Pockets investing strategies, you'll see how My Real Estate Exit Strategy was born.

I have people reading my books all around the world. It's impossible for me to know exactly where you are located. You know in the real estate profession the motto is "All Real Estate is Local, " so it's logical to assume as a professional real estate agent, you know your local real estate market. I would suggest you use that information to your advantage when buying property for yourself.

I'm not a financial advisor. I'm just a real estate agent just like you. I'm just suggesting if you're a pretty savvy real estate agent, buy a piece of property once every year or two. Start your real estate empire one closed transaction at a time. What I mean by this is after every closed transaction, put a little bit aside for your future Investments.

On the other hand, if you're an agent that's comfortable helping other people buy and sell real estate, but would like to take the extra steps learning the proper ways to build your investment property portfolio with proven systems and techniques, I would suggest checking out the Bigger Pockets YouTube channel. If their videos and techniques pique your curiosity, then go to their website at BiggerPockets.com. They have an abundance of information, blogs, and free video courses. You can sign up for free or get their paid subscription. I do not get anything if you sign up for their paid program. I'm just sharing with you a very good source of information.

I also suggest reading and studying as much investment information as you can from proven seasoned investors such as Robert Kiyosaki. Robert has a YouTube channel and a podcast with a wealth of information that not only will help you invest in real estate but also how to protect it from lawsuits and the taxman.

Let me ask you another serious question. How would your financial future look if you took the steps to safeguard your livelihood by buying just a few income properties and the real estate market and the economy tanked? How would your finances look? Not so great right, but not devastating, right? The point is that you're in a better position now because you took action than if you did not take any action. Wouldn't you agree?

Most of us are distracted by the hamster wheel of life and never taking the time to really sit down and focus on our financial future. I mean life gets in the way sometimes and we make crazy stupid mistakes. That's life! We need to make a lot of mistakes so we can learn from them and move forward. When I first got into real estate, I sold my successful School Bus Company. A few years later, I had one of my best years in real estate and I did not budget my money correctly. I had a few deals fall out of contract and it just devastated me financially. I had to start driving the bus again to make ends meet.

But like Rocky, I did not give up. I kept pushing forward. I learned from my mistakes and started budgeting my money with more accountability. I ignored the naysayers. I work hard each and every day. For a long while, my schedule looked like this: drive the school bus all day, make a quick stop at the house to take a shower and change my clothes, and then off to the office. I was working hard doing something productive each and every day to get closer back to where I once was which was cutting off the bus and devoting my full time into what I love most, **Selling Real Estate**.

No matter where you are in the real estate evolution process, you need to understand that life is going to get in the way. You're going to make mistakes. Learn from those mistakes. Develop a mindset that you can do anything in real estate you want to. Learn and listen to other proven top agents and how they became successful. Pay attention to how they overcame the mistakes they made, so you can avoid them. I do not know you, but I believe in you. Why you may ask? Because if you didn't want to be a better real estate agent, you would have never picked up this book. That's why I know you're going to kick some real estate assets!

A little side note:

I know we all have busy lives and it's hard to keep up with current events and things related to our business. Do you remember when I said my father taught me about preparing for the worst-case scenario? That also goes for looking into the future, as much as possible. In this way, you can prepare yourself for what may be ahead when possible.

I know I will probably get a lot of flak for this, and I was debating on if I should put this in the book, but I feel I should share my thoughts and you can make your own decisions regarding your future. This is just my opinion and you will probably hear it from me first because you will not hear it in the regular news media.

Cryptocurrency and blockchain will be a part of our financial future faster than you think. The President and World banking leaders are all talking about a Level Playing Field. The President's Executive order for Faster Payments Task Force, International Stock Exchange, New York Stock Exchange, Fidelity, and the NASDAQ among others are soon-to-be adding cryptocurrencies to their exchanges.

You probably noticed fewer and fewer Bank branches. With blockchain and Ripple technology, you will not need physical Bank to handle your banking transactions. All you will need is your phone. Transactions that once took up to two weeks will take seconds anywhere around the world. The technology is so scary you can make payments with facial recognition or Live Scan using your fingerprint.

I'm informing you of this information because in my opinion, at the time of this writing 2019, real estate as we know it will no longer exist in 3 to 5 years. You can see it changing as we speak. Different properties around the world are being tokenized and recorded on the blockchain. Thanks to Natalia Karayaneva and her company called Propy Inc., they are solving problems purchasing properties across borders. Propy Inc. is the world's first International real estate Marketplace.

This is a very exciting time to be a real estate agent. But we also need to be on top of the technology of our chosen field. Closing transactions within 30 to 45 days will soon be a distant memory. Using blockchain technology, we are already seeing real estate transactions being closed in a few days. Soon it will be within a few hours or a few minutes. Keep an eye on this technology, so you will not be left behind. In the worst-case scenario, make up your mind to purchase investment properties for your exit strategy, so you can have that passive income and hedge against anything the future may hold.

Remember this: "No matter which way the economy goes or the evolution of technology or innovation. People will always need a place to live and pay rent!"

Final Thoughts

I would like to tell you right now, thank you for purchasing my book. This book will not do you any good if you don't utilize the information within it. Do not let this book sit on your shelf and collect dust. Use this book as your Real Estate Survival Guide. These tactics are your year-round Real Estate Survival Guide.

A successful Real Estate Agent can make more than most doctors, lawyers, and even surgeons. We have a license to sell. If you work smart, hard, and are consistent with your prospecting, the sky's the limit. I read in Forbes Magazine that the highest-paid salespeople, "sell with a purpose" or "sell with a noble purpose". They are not selling to get rich or famous but to help people. What is your purpose when you are selling Real Estate? What is your WHY?

Whatever your purpose is, let that drive you towards success, have it yank you out of bed in the morning, and allow it to destroy self-doubt and avoidance behavior. Let it guide you through your prospecting calls during the day. Depending on the individual, it takes anywhere from sixty to seventy-five days to develop a habit. Studies have shown that once that habit is ingrained in you, even if you don't want to do it, your inner drive will compel you to continue doing it. There have been times when I did not want to go to the office and prospect, but I was so conditioned on doing it. I still went. Once I was on the phone making calls, I was glad I came in.

Your habit will drive you when the days of your fire and passion run low. I believe in you. You have it in yourself to be a successful Real Estate Agent. I know I talk a lot about mindset throughout this book, but sometimes we need a kick in the pants. If you let that drunken monkey in your mind to control your success, you will never succeed.

So if you need a little help fighting the drunken monkey, practicing your scripts and dialogues, or you would just like to mastermind with other Real Estate Agents, I have started a new Facebook group called **Real Estate Agents That Hustle** - https://www.facebook.com/groups/RealEstateAgentsThatHustle/. I invite you to join us, so we can help you mold your Real Estate career for success.

I would like to congratulate you for taking the time out of your busy schedule to read this book. I really appreciate it. I know many Agents struggle in Real Estate, myself included. I wanted to put together something that will benefit fellow Agents and their families.

If I can give you the information that helped me in my business and help you with yours, that would be the best gift for me and my family. I hope and pray that the information in this book will increase your business tenfold. If it has, please contact me and let me know. No matter where you are in the world, what race or religion, no matter what language you speak, I want to hear from you. From the bottom of my heart, from my family to yours, may God richly bless you.

Thank You All

I would like to say thank you for spending your hard-earned money purchasing this book and most of all, for taking the time to learn the materials inside it. If this book or audiobook helps you in any way please leave a review. We all need help from time to time, so I've included a few gifts for you.

Here are links to all my Real Estate video courses. This is over 3 hours of video content for less than $10 each. This is my way of saying "Thank You"!

Real Estate Listing Mastery 101
http://williejmayenterprises.com/thankyou101

New Real Estate Agent Business Plan
http://williejmayenterprises.com/bizplan

Open House Master Class for Real Estate Agents
http://williejmayenterprises.com/openhouse

Real Estate Agents Pre-List Package
http://williejmayenterprises.com/prelistpackage

www.ingramcontent.com/pod-product-compliance
Lightning Source LLC
Chambersburg PA
CBHW070339220526
45467CB00001B/174